AS/A-LEVEL YEAR 1
STUDENT GUIDE

EDEXCEL

Politics

UK politics

Neil McNaughton

Series editor: Eric Magee

HODDER
EDUCATION
AN HACHETTE UK COMPANY

Hodder Education, an Hachette UK company, Blenheim Court, George Street, Banbury, Oxfordshire OX16 5BH

Orders

Bookpoint Ltd, 130 Park Drive, Milton Park, Abingdon, Oxfordshire OX14 4SB

tel: 01235 827720

fax: 01235 400401

e-mail: education@bookpoint.co.uk

Lines are open 9.00 a.m.–5.00 p.m., Monday to Saturday, with a 24-hour message answering service. You can also order through the Hodder Education website: www.hoddereducation.co.uk

© Neil McNaughton 2017

ISBN 978-1-4718-9308-7

First printed 2017

Impression number 5 4 3 2 1

Year 2021 2020 2019 2018 2017

This Guide has been written specifically to support students preparing for the Edexcel AS and A-level Politics examinations. The content has been neither approved nor endorsed by Edexcel and remains the sole responsibility of the author.

Typeset by Aptara Inc., India

Printed in Italy

Hachette UK's policy is to use papers that are natural, renewable and recyclable products and made from wood grown in sustainable forests. The logging and manufacturing processes are expected to conform to the environmental regulations of the country of origin.

Contents

Content Guidance

Questions and Answers

■Getting the most from this book

Exam-style questions

Commentary on the questions

Tips on what you need to do to gain full marks, indicated by the icon ⓔ

Sample student answers

Practise the questions, then look at the student answers that follow.

Commentary on sample student answers

Read the comments (preceded by the icon ⓔ) showing how many marks each answer would be awarded in the exam and exactly where marks are gained or lost.

Voting behaviour and the media

Question 2

Evaluate the relative importance of different demographic factors in voting behaviour.

(30 marks)

You must consider this view and the alternative to this view in a balanced way.

ⓔ At the beginning you need to establish which demographic factors you are going to examine. You should only attempt a question like this if you have command of some key data to use as evidence. Vague generalisations will gain some credit, but not as much as hard data. Using data as evidence, you need to identify which factors are more important than others. You should then attempt an overall evaluation of what the most decisive factors are.

Student A

In this essay I will be looking at a variety of demographic factors including social class, age, gender, ethnicity and region. There is no doubt that class remains the most important factor, but some of the other factors are important too. The only factor that has little importance is gender because men and women pretty much vote in the same way. There is no difference between them. First I will look at class. ⓐ

Class used to be the most important factor with two thirds of the working class supporting Labour and even more of the middle class supporting the Conservatives. Now, however, class is less important. There are many more deviant voters who do not vote the way their class suggests they would. Only about 40% of people vote the way their class would suggest.

Having said all this, the best indicator of how people will vote is their ethnic identity. Black and Asian British voters are far more likely to support Labour than the Conservatives. The only group that is different are Muslims whose voting is mixed between the main parties.

It is therefore clear that class remains a key factor, but it is not as important as ethnicity and it is now closely rivalled by region as a factor. One of the reasons for this is class dealignment. Fewer and fewer people identify themselves with one class or another. This means that the link between class and voting is getting weaker. ⓑ

ⓔ 15/30 marks awarded. This is a reasonable essay with a good structure and coverage of the main issues. It suffers from the problem of being somewhat out of date, using 2015 figures rather than 2017. ⓐ The introduction promises a well-constructed answer. However, it has one major weakness and one lesser weakness. The major weakness is its lack of hard statistics as evidence. The statements made are broadly accurate but are too generalised. ⓑ and ⓒ both lack hard data. The other weakness is that there is no mention of referendums. The demographic factors in the Scottish and EU referendums were especially interesting and informative. ⓓ The conclusion is fine, though the material on class dealignment should be in the body of the answer.

ⓔ AO1: 4/10 marks, AO2: 5/10 marks, AO3: 6/10 marks

■About this book

The aim of this Student Guide is to prepare you for the Edexcel A-level Paper 1, UK Politics. This paper comprises a third of the Politics A-level, and all of the topics covered in this guide could be examined in the exam. It is therefore vital that you are familiar and confident with all the material.

The **Content Guidance** section covers all the topics largely in the order that they appear on the Edexcel AS/A-level specification, UK politics section. You are strongly advised to have a copy of the most recent version of the specification to refer to as you go through the topics. There are four main topics:

■ Democracy and participation
■ Political parties
■ Electoral systems
■ Voting behaviour and the media

Each of these sections is further divided into two or three subsections.

You should use the Content Guidance section to ensure you are familiar with all the key concepts and terms, statistics, issues and arguments, and have a range of relevant examples you can quote in your answers to show you are aware of the relative significance of these principles and concepts.

The **Questions & Answers** section provides an opportunity for you to hone your exam technique and to become familiar with the skills and structures that examiners are looking for.

This guide does not provide a complete range of examples or go into full detail, so you should use it alongside other resources such as class notes, the *Edexcel AS/A-level UK Government and Politics* textbook by Neil McNaughton and articles in *Politics Review* (both published by Hodder Education). You should also use websites such as the BBC, TotalPolitics.com, The Times Red Box and www.politics.co.uk to keep up to date with current news.

Content Guidance

■ Democracy and participation

Democracy refers to a society where the people have real influence over the political decisions that will affect them. It also means that government is accountable to the people. The key features of any democracy, as the term is generally understood, are as follows:

- The people have influence over political decision making.
- The government is accountable to the people.
- There are free and fair elections so that the government is considered to be **legitimate**.
- Different beliefs, political parties and political associations are tolerated.
- The media are free and independent.
- The rights of citizens are legally guaranteed.
- There are legal limits to the powers of government, established by a constitution and an independent judiciary.

The two main types of democracy are representative and direct democracy.

Legitimacy The idea that a government has a right to govern, normally granted through elections, implying that it has the consent of the people.

Representative and direct democracy

Direct democracy

Direct democracy is a system where the people themselves make important political decisions. The modern form involves the use of referendums. The use of direct democracy through referendums is controversial. Table 1 summarises the main arguments for and against direct democracy:

Direct democracy A form of democracy where people make political decisions directly instead of their elected representatives. In modern direct democracy, referendums are used to resolve key political and constitutional issues.

Table 1 Arguments for and against direct democracy

Arguments for	Arguments against
It is the purest form of democracy. The people's voice is clearly heard.	It can lead to the 'tyranny of the majority', whereby the winning majority simply ignores the interests of the minority. Elected representatives can mediate between the interests of the majority and minorities.
It can avoid delay and deadlock within the political system.	The people may be too easily swayed by short-term, emotional appeals by charismatic individuals. (The great philosopher Plato criticised direct democracy on these grounds.)
The fact that people are making a decision gives it great legitimacy.	Some issues may be too complex for the ordinary citizen to understand.

Representative democracy

In contrast to direct democracy, representative democracy refers to a system where the people are represented by others. Representatives are usually elected, but can also include pressure groups and social movements. In the UK there are various forms of representation:

- **Party representation.** Political parties create political programmes, including party manifestos at election time. If elected they seek to implement these programmes.
- **Constituency representation.** It is expected that elected representatives should represent the interests and concerns of their constituency at local, regional and national levels.
- **Functional representation.** Specific groups in society may be represented by pressure groups or by elected representatives. Typical groups include occupations, age groups, ethnic minorities, disabled people and social minorities. They may be represented by sectional pressure groups, some MPs and peers.
- **Causal representation.** Various campaign groups represent people with specific beliefs and concerns. For example, environmentalists, anti-capitalists, peace campaigners, animal rights supporters, transport groups.
- **Social representation.** This is a principle that representative organisations, notably parliament and other elected assemblies, are socially representative of the whole population. This means, for example, 50% women, an appropriate proportion of ethnic minorities, and different social classes and age characteristics.

Representation
A democratic principle whereby the people expect to be represented to government by elected individuals, parties or other associations.

Party manifesto A set of political proposals, forming a political programme, presented to the electorate at each election. Voters can base their party choice on which manifesto they prefer.

Representative and direct democracy compared

The distinctions between representative and direct democracy are as follows:
- With direct democracy the people themselves make political decisions, while with representative democracy decisions are made by elected members of councils, assemblies and parliaments.
- With direct democracy decisions are made by referendum whereas with representative democracy decisions are made by government and elected assemblies.
- With direct democracy the people decide on single issues while in representative democracy people choose between full political programmes at elections rather than on single issues.

Advantages and disadvantages of direct and representative democracy

Table 2 summarises the main advantages and disadvantages of direct democracy.

Table 2 An assessment of direct democracy

Advantages	Disadvantages
It gives legitimacy to political decisions if the people themselves make them.	Issues may be too complex for people to judge.
It is a decisive form of decision making and avoids excessive debate within the political system.	The people may be swayed in their judgement by emotional appeals and false claims and information. They may not have enough information to make a rational decision.
Decisions made by the people cannot be overturned by political leaders.	Representatives are democratically accountable for their decisions, which helps to make them act responsibly. The people cannot be held accountable to themselves.

> **Exam tip**
>
> Use examples to illustrate the points you make in exam answers. This is especially important in questions about direct democracy and referendums. Examples of referendums can be found on page 10.

Table 3 summarises the main advantages and disadvantages of representative democracy.

Table 3 An assessment of representative democracy

Advantages	Disadvantages
Representatives may have expert knowledge and experience which the general public do not possess.	Elected representatives may be more interested in party politics than in the national interest. In general, parties may exercise too much control over their elected members.
Representatives are likely to be more rational and less likely to be swayed by emotional appeals.	There is no guarantee that representatives, whether elected or not, accurately reflect the views of those whom they claim to represent.
Representatives are democratically accountable and therefore should behave in a responsible way.	The UK electoral system produces a highly unrepresentative result.

> **Knowledge check 1**
>
> Identify the following:
>
> - a pressure group that represents elderly people
> - the name given to those elected to the Welsh Assembly
> - the name given to those elected at local government level
> - the subject of the national referendum held in the UK in 2011

The case for reform of representative democracy

The UK democracy is largely representative in nature. However, there are a number of problems with the system of democracy. This is sometimes described as a 'democratic deficit'. The main problems associated with democracy in the UK include:

- Half of the UK parliament is not elected — the House of Lords.
- General elections produce unrepresentative outcomes. Governments may achieve an overall majority of the *seats* in parliament, but they never achieve a majority of the total votes. The Conservative government elected in 2015 won less than 38% of the national vote.
- Some parties, such as the Liberal Democrats and the Green Party, are under-represented because of the electoral system, while others, such as Labour and the Conservatives, are over-represented.
- MPs are subject to strong party discipline and so are not independent when voting and expressing their views.
- Governments are democratically accountable at elections, but it is said they are not accountable enough between elections.

Democratic deficit A term expressing the belief that the UK political system has a number of faults which make it less than fully democratic.

Table 4 summarises the UK's democratic deficit and shows the positive and negative aspects of representative democracy in the UK. It also shows the proposals that have been made to address these.

Table 4 Representative democracy in the UK assessed

Democratic feature	Positives	Negatives	Reform proposals
Elections	All over 18 can vote. There is little electoral fraud and strong legal safeguards exist to prevent fraud.	In general elections, the first-past-the-post system distorts support for parties and produces an unrepresentative House of Commons.	Reform the electoral system and introduce some form of proportional representation.
Parliament	The House of Commons can hold the government to account.	The House of Lords is unelected.	Introduce an elected second chamber.
Pressure and campaign groups	People are free to form political associations.	Governments have power to resist pressure if they have a parliamentary majority.	Proportional representation in the UK parliament would make MPs more independent and see more groups being represented in parliament.
Distribution of power	Devolution has spread power away from London to the national regions.	Devolved governments in Scotland, Wales and Northern Ireland have limited powers.	Grant further powers to devolved governments.
Public participation	People are free to vote, to stand for office and to express political views.	Turnouts at elections remain low by historical standards, while party membership is also lower than typically before the 1990s.	A fairer election system might encourage more voting. Widen the franchise to 16+ voters and perhaps make voting compulsory.
Protection of rights and liberties	Strong in the UK. The country is signed up to the European Convention on Human Rights (ECHR) and the courts enforce it. The Supreme Court and the judiciary enforce the rule of law.	Parliament is sovereign, which means that it can remove or weaken the protection of rights.	Make parliament subject to the ECHR.

Mandate and manifesto

Representative democracy in the UK should be understood in terms of the doctrine of **mandate and manifesto**. Their meanings are as follows:

- **Manifesto** refers to the political proposals put forward by each political party at the time of an election. This is used as the basis for the judgement of voters in choosing between parties.

Mandate and manifesto
The democratic doctrine that an elected government has a mandate, or authority, to put into practice all the proposals in its last election manifesto.

- **Mandate** refers to the authority given to an elected government when it wins an election. The mandate it has is based on its election manifesto. The government has authority to carry out all the proposals in its last manifesto. The mandate also helps to make government accountable.

The doctrine of mandate and manifesto has the following weaknesses and flaws:

- Most of the electorate do not read manifestos and have only a generalised knowledge of what is contained in them.
- The doctrine assumes the majority of the electorate approves of *all* the details of the manifesto; this is clearly unlikely.
- In the UK governments are elected on a minority of the popular vote (only 38% in 2015) so most of the electorate vote *against* the government's manifesto.
- If no single party wins a majority, as occurred in 2010, the resulting coalition has no clear mandate.
- Unforeseen events may prevent the government carrying out its manifesto.

Political participation

There are a number of ways in which people can participate in politics. The main examples are:

- voting in elections and referendums
- being a member of a political party
- being an especially active member of a political party
- standing for election to public office at local, regional or national level
- becoming a member of a pressure group or campaign group
- becoming involved in political campaigns online, including signing e-petitions

Tables 5 and 6 show the turnout at referendums and general elections in the UK.

Table 5 Turnout at UK referendums

Year	Subject of referendum		Turnout (%)
1997–98	Devolution to: ■ Scotland ■ Wales ■ Northern Ireland		60.4 50.1 81.0
1998	Should London have an elected mayor?		34.1
2011	The introduction of the AV electoral system		42.2
2014	Scottish independence		84.6
2016	British membership of the EU		72.2

Table 6 Turnout at UK general elections

Year	Turnout (%)	Year	Turnout (%)
1950	83.9	2001	59.4
1964	77.1	2005	61.4
1979	76.0	2010	65.1
1992	77.7	2015	66.1
1997	71.4	2017	68.7

Knowledge check 2

Study Tables 5 and 6.

- What can you say about the long-term trend in UK general elections?
- What can you say about the typical differences between turnout at referendums and turnout at elections?
- The general elections in 1950, 1964, 1992, 2010, 2015 and 2017 were all very close. Do the figures suggest an effect on turnout?

It is sometimes said that the UK is suffering from a **participation crisis**. This suggests that there is a decline in the number of people who are participating in politics in various ways. However, the evidence varies. In some ways participation is declining, but in others it is increasing (as shown in Table 7).

Table 7 Does the UK have a participation crisis?

Evidence that it does	Evidence that it does not
Turnout at elections has been low in recent years, despite a small recovery in 2010–17, and very variable at referendums.	Several e-petitions have had very high response rates (e.g. for a second EU referendum in 2016: 3.8 million and against a road pricing scheme in 2007: 1.8 million).
Membership of parties has declined significantly over the past 30 years.	Membership of the Labour, Liberal Democratic, Green and Scottish National parties grew in 2015–17.
There is a good deal of **disillusion and apathy**, especially among the young who have become disengaged from party politics.	Young people are increasingly involved in pressure groups, social movements and online campaigns.
Support for the two main parties is in decline.	UKIP has attracted many new, first-time voters, although its membership tell again after 2017.

The franchise and suffrage

Milestones in the widening of the franchise

- Between 1832 (The Great Reform Act) and 1928 the franchise was gradually extended.
- In 1832 the franchise was extended to about 8% of the adult population.
- In 1867 and 1884 the franchise was extended to most men, but not women.
- In 1918 the vote was given to married women over 30.
- In 1928 the vote was given to all women.
- In 1969 the vote was extended to all adults over 18 instead of over 21.
- In 2016 16- and 17-year olds were granted the vote in Scotland.

Suffragettes and suffragists

The suffragettes used both legal and illegal methods to campaign for votes for women. The suffragists stuck to legal methods. Their significance is:

- Contemporary pressure groups can learn a great deal from the methods of the votes for women movement.

Participation crisis A belief, common in the twenty-first century, that political participation in the UK has declined so much that it has become a threat to the democratic health of the country.

Disillusion and apathy A modern development suggesting that a high proportion of the electorate are disillusioned with the performance of governments and the parties and that this leads to apathy, notably low turnouts at elections.

Suffrage A term that refers to the right to vote. The term 'franchise' is an alternative.

- They illustrate the fact that illegal methods can work in political campaigns.
- They were a key stage in the development of feminism though they did not describe themselves as feminists.

Current issues in the franchise and voting

There are three main issues concerned with voting in the UK today:

- whether 16- and 17-year olds should be given the vote
- whether voting should be made compulsory
- what ways can be devised to encourage more people to vote other than making it compulsory

The debate about votes for 16- and 17-year-olds is outlined in Table 8.

Knowledge check 3

Outline **four** ways in which people participate in politics in the UK.

Table 8 Should 16- and 17-year-olds be given the right to vote?

Arguments in favour	Arguments against
With the spread of citizenship education, young people are now better informed about politics than ever before.	16- and 17-year-olds are too young to be able to make rational judgements.
Voting turnout among the 18–24-year-old age group is very low. This may encourage more people to vote and become engaged with politics.	Many issues are too complex for younger people to understand.
The internet and social media now enable young people to be better informed about politics.	Few people in this age group pay tax so they have a lower stake in society.
If one is old enough to serve in the army, get married or pay tax, one should be old enough to vote.	

The debate about whether voting should be compulsory is outlined in Table 9.

Table 9 Should the UK introduce compulsory voting?

Arguments for	Arguments against
It may force more voters, especially the young, to make themselves more informed about political issues.	It is a civil liberties violation. Many argue it is a basic right *not* to take part.
By increasing turnout it will give greater democratic legitimacy to the party or individual(s) who win an election.	Many voters are not well informed and yet they will be voting, so there will be ill-informed participation.
By ensuring that more sections of society are involved, decision makers will have to ensure that policies will address the concerns of all parts of society, not just those who typically vote in larger numbers.	It will involve large amounts of public expenditure to administer and enforce the system.
It can be argued that voting is a civic duty so citizens should be obliged to carry out that duty.	It will probably favour larger parties against small parties. This is because less-informed citizens will vote and they may have only heard of better-known parties and candidates.

The ways that have been proposed to increase turnout other than by making voting compulsory include the following:

- Make registering to vote more convenient, especially online.
- Possibly introduce online voting.
- Introduce weekend voting.
- Encourage more political education in schools.
- Votes for 16- and 17-year-olds might encourage more voting among the young.
- It should be added that reforming the electoral system might work to increase voting. With some form of proportional representation fewer votes would be seen as wasted.

Pressure groups and other influences

Types of pressure group

Pressure groups are usually classified in four ways. These are:

1 Sectional (or interest) groups. These represent the interests of a particular section of society such as occupational groups, professions, age groups, groups receiving welfare, people with medical conditions, business and industrial groups.

2 Promotional (or issue) groups. These do not represent the interests of a section of society but represent an issue which affects the community at local, regional, national or global level.

3 Insider groups. These have close links with government or parliament or local and regional bodies. They are mostly sectional groups. They are regularly consulted and have inside influence.

4 Outsider groups. These do not have insider influence on government and other decision makers. They are mostly promotional groups which put pressure on decision makers by mobilising broad public opinion.

Pressure group
An association or movement that campaigns either to further the interests of a section of society, or to further a particular cause or issue.

Knowledge check 4

Consider these prominent pressure groups. How would you classify each one?

- Greenpeace
- Confederation of British Industry
- NSPCC
- National Farmers' Union
- Countryside Alliance

Pressure group methods and factors in success or failure

Pressure groups experience extremely varying degrees of success and failure. Success means promoting favourable legislation in parliament and preventing unfavourable legislation. It can also mean simply raising public awareness of an issue or persuading government to place an issue on the political agenda. Two areas of pressure group activity should be considered. These are the methods typically used (see Table 10) and the factors that contribute to their success or otherwise (see Table 11).

Table 10 Campaigning methods

Pressure group	Aims	Methods
Plane Stupid	To prevent airport expansions	■ Invading airports and blocking flights ■ Occupying airport terminals ■ Blocking entrances to airports ■ Delaying Heathrow expansion with a judicial review case ■ Organising e-petitions
British Medical Association (BMA)	To force government to withdraw a new contract for junior hospital doctors	■ Regular withdrawal of labour for routine operations and treatments
UK Finance (formerly) British Bankers Association	To prevent government imposing excessive regulations on banks	■ Lobbying ministers and sympathetic MPs and peers
Friends of the Earth	Promoting environmental protection	■ Public campaigns to attract members ■ Research and publicity campaigns to highlight environmental problems ■ Lobbying ministers and parliament
Liberty	Protecting citizens' rights and freedoms	■ Initiating court cases against public bodies and government (judicial reviews mostly) when it is felt rights are under threat

Exam tip

When discussing pressure groups, always quote as many examples as you can to illustrate your answer.

Table 11 What makes some pressure groups more successful than others?

Success factors	Failure factors
Size. Many members and/or followers suggests more pressure on government and possibly more available funds. Example: **Age UK**.	**Small size.** Such groups suffer from lack of active support and usually funds. Example: **Local environmental protection groups**.
Finance. With ample funds a group can mount successful campaigns and use publicity. Example: **UK Finance**.	**Government opposition.** Sometimes groups and their aims fall out of favour with government. Example: **Trade unions and the Conservatives** after 2015.
Strategic position in society. Groups that are vital to society have more political leverage. Example: **British Medical Association (BMA)**.	**Adverse public opinion.** Some groups fail to capture the public imagination. Example: Pro-smoking group, **Forest**.
Public opinion. Some campaign groups enjoy the widespread support of the public. Example: **Action on Smoking and Health (ASH)**.	**Countervailing forces.** Groups may fail because they face powerful adversaries. Example: **Anti-fracking groups** are opposed by powerful energy companies.
Government support. Some groups have views which accord with government policy. Example: **Child Poverty Action Group** (when Labour was in power).	

Pressure group case studies

When undertaking a case study of a pressure group you should research the following:

- If it is a sectional group, whom does it represent?
- What are its objectives?
- What are its main methods?
- What notable successes has it achieved?
- What are the reasons for its successes and failures?

Pressure groups and democracy

A key issue concerns whether pressure groups are a positive or negative force in a democracy. In general they are seen as a key aspect of a **pluralist** society and they do disperse power and influence more widely, but they can also concentrate influence in a few hands. This debate is show in more detail in Table 12.

Table 12 Do pressure groups enhance or threaten democracy?

Ways in which they enhance democracy	Ways in which they may threaten democracy
Pressure groups help to disperse power and influence more widely.	Some pressure groups are elitist and tend to concentrate power in too few hands.
Pressure groups educate the public about important political issues.	Influential pressure groups may distort information in their own interests.
Pressure groups give people more opportunities to participate in politics without having to sacrifice too much of their time and attention.	Pressure groups that are internally undemocratic may not accurately represent the views of their members and supporters.
Pressure groups can promote and protect the interests and rights of minorities.	Finance is a key factor in political influence so groups that are wealthy may wield a disproportionate amount of influence.
Pressure groups help to call government to account by publicising the effects of policy.	

Think tanks, lobby groups and corporations

Some important lobby groups (**lobbyists**) and **think tanks** that have considerable influence on decision makers are listed below:

Neutral think tanks

- **ResPublica** — general policy issues
- **Chatham House** — international affairs
- **Centre for Social Justice** — policy on welfare issues

'Left-wing' think tanks

- **Fabian Society** — issues concerning social justice and equality
- **Institute for Public Policy Research** — various left-wing policy ideas

'Right-wing' think tanks

- **Institute of Economic Affairs** — promoting free market solutions to economic issues
- **Centre for Policy Studies** — promoting ideas popular in the premiership of Margaret Thatcher

Pluralism This refers to the state of a society and a political system. Pluralism implies that power is widely dispersed, that many parties and other political groups are allowed to flourish and that a wide range of views and beliefs are tolerated.

Elitism A feature of society and the political system which suggests that some groups, associations and other business enterprises may wield a considerable amount of influence. In other words, power and influence are concentrated in their particular hands rather than being widely dispersed.

Lobbyists Individuals and organisations that act on behalf of companies, industries, pressure groups and other causes by seeking to influence government in policy and law making.

Think tank A colloquial term which refers to research organisations that produce information and opinions about policy issues. Some are funded by government, some by political parties and some by private enterprise.

'Liberal' think tanks

- **Liberty** — promoting issues concerning the protection of rights and liberties
- **Reform** — concerning policies on welfare, public services and economic management

Examples of corporations that wield considerable political influence include:

- all major banks
- all major motor manufacturers operating in the UK
- major media groups
- energy companies

Exam tip

When discussing democracy in any context, it is important to consider how well dispersed power and influence are — well dispersed in a pluralist system, or more concentrated in a few hands in an elitist system. It is generally held that, in a healthy democracy, power, influence and knowledge are widely dispersed.

Rights in context

Milestones in the development of rights in the UK

Three key stages in the development of rights protection in the UK are:

- **The Human Rights Act 1998.** This had the effect of bringing the European Convention on Human Rights into UK law. It strengthened the protection of a whole range of rights and liberties. It made civil liberties a firm part of UK law.
- **The Freedom of Information Act 2000.** This Act gives citizens the right to view information held by any public body in two categories — first, information held about him- or herself and, second, information which may be of public interest. The only exception is information that might threaten national security if published.
- **The Equality Act 2010.** This replaced several existing pieces of legislation establishing rights in the UK. The Act outlaws any kind of discrimination on the grounds of gender, ethnicity, religion, disablement and sexual orientation.

The issue of how well rights are currently protected in the UK is much disputed. The debate on this issue is shown in Table 13.

Table 13 The protection of rights in the UK: strengths and weaknesses

Strengths	Weaknesses
There is a strong common law tradition.	Common law can be vague and disputed. It can also be set aside by parliamentary statutes.
The UK is subject to the European Convention on Human Rights.	Parliament remains sovereign and so can ignore the ECHR or can even repeal the Human Rights Act.
The judiciary has a reputation for being independent and upholding the rule of law even against the expressed wishes of government and parliament. Civil rights are therefore virtually guaranteed.	There is increasing pressure on government, as a result of international terrorism, to curtail rights in the interests of national security. The right to privacy, the rights of association and expression as well as freedom from imprisonment without trial are all threatened.

Civil liberties Those rights and freedoms which cannot be abused or reduced by any public body. They include such examples as freedom of thought, expression, association and movement.

Civil rights Rights that citizens enjoy in relation to government and the law. Specifically the term refers to rights such as voting, standing for office and being politically active generally. It also means the right not to be discriminated against by the law. It is therefore an element in the principle of the rule of law.

Obligations/responsibilities

As well as having rights, UK citizens are considered to have responsibilities or obligations towards the state. These are open to a certain amount of debate. The lists below show which responsibilities are not in dispute and which can be considered to be responsibilities but are uncertain.

Clear citizens' responsibilities

- To obey the law
- To pay taxes
- To undertake jury service when required

Disputed citizens' responsibilities in the UK

- To serve in the armed forces when the country is under attack
- To vote in elections and referendums
- To respect the rights of all other citizens
- To respect the dominant values of the society

> **Exam tip**
>
> When discussing rights in any context, it is important to distinguish between individual rights, which are largely protected in law, and collective rights, which are usually protected by government and parliament.

Individual and collective rights

Problems can arise when the individual rights of citizens conflict with the rights of the community *as a whole*. In some cases these conflicts have no answer. They remain difficult political issues.

Table 14 Conflicts between individual and collective (community) rights

Individual rights	Conflicting collective rights
Freedom of expression	The right of religious groups not to have their beliefs satirised or questioned
The right to privacy	The right of the community to be protected from terrorism by security services who may listen in to private communications
The right to press freedom	The right of public figures to keep their private lives private
The right to demonstrate in public places (right to association and free movement) and thus cause disruption	The right of the community to their own freedom of movement
The right to strike in pursuit of pay and employment rights	The right of the community to expect good service from public servants who are paid from taxation

Content Guidance

Summary

When you have completed this topic you should have a thorough knowledge of the following information and issues:

- the distinctions between direct and representative democracy
- the relative merits of direct and representative democracy
- how to assess direct democracy
- how to assess representative democracy
- the nature of the doctrine of mandate and manifesto
- the weaknesses in the doctrine of mandate and manifesto
- the ways in which people participate in politics
- the extent to which the UK suffers from a participation crisis
- the nature of the franchise
- the issues surrounding the current state of the franchise
- the nature and classification of pressure groups
- factors affecting the success and failure of pressure groups
- the role of pressure groups in a democracy
- the ways in which various groups enjoy influence in the political system
- the ways in which rights and liberties are protected in the UK
- the nature of the conflicts between individual and collective rights

In addition, you should have gathered appropriate information to help you answer the following wide-ranging questions:

1 How democratic is the UK?
2 How might political participation be increased in the UK?
3 To what extent is direct democracy preferable to representative democracy?
4 To what extent is power in the UK dispersed or concentrated?
5 How effectively are rights protected in the UK?

■ Political parties

Political parties explained

Functions and features of political parties

The functions of **political parties** are:

- They exist to convert political ideas and aspirations into policies that may be adopted within the political system and ultimately become decisions. They convert political demands into practical political programmes of action.
- They provide organised opportunities for people to participate meaningfully in politics.
- They recruit people who can stand for election to representative institutions at local, regional and national levels.
- They manage election campaigns, presenting the electorate with choices between sets of policies.
- They educate the general public about political issues.
- When in opposition rather than government they call government to account.

The features of political parties are:

- The members hold broadly similar political views.
- They seek either power or an influence on those who hold power.
- They usually have some kind of organisation whose purpose is to develop policies and recruit candidates for election.
- They have some kind of formal membership.

Mandate and manifesto

The concepts of mandate and manifesto are critical to an understanding of how parties work and how they fit into the context of UK politics. The terms mean the following:

- **Manifesto.** This is a document that sets out a party's policies at the time of a general election. The contents are both policy aspirations and commitments. It is expected that all the party's candidates subscribe to the same manifesto unless they openly declare some variations. If the party wins the election and gains power, it is expected that it should carry out its manifesto commitments as far as possible and will be judged on the basis of how successfully it does so.
- **Mandate.** If a party wins the election and takes power, it has a mandate or authority) to carry out *all* its manifesto commitments. This is a key democratic aspect of party politics in the UK.

Left- and right-wing politics

Table 15 shows the kinds of policies associated with **left-wing** and **right-wing** political ideas:

Political party An association of people who share similar political views and who seek political representation or power in order to put those views into practice.

Left wing A political position, often associated with socialism and social democracy, mainly concerned with creating more equality between different groups in society.

Right wing A political position, often associated with conservatism. It involves low taxation, low state involvement, the protection of free markets and an acceptance of inequality in society.

Table 15 The distinction between left- and right-wing political ideas

Left-wing ideas	Right-wing ideas
Redistributing income from rich to poor through taxation and welfare	Low levels of taxation to encourage private enterprise and create incentives to work
Strong support for the welfare state	Acceptance of private sector involvement in the provision of public services
Support for workers' rights and trade union power	The state should not interfere with the working of the economy save for exceptional circumstances
The state should support industries which are vital to society and the economy	Support for free markets in goods, finance and labour, including reducing trade union power
Support for measures designed to create equality of opportunity	Keeping welfare benefits relatively low as an incentive for people to find work and not become too dependent on the state
A stress on equal rights for all groups in society	A strong position on law and order
	A stress on national unity and patriotism

The policies of political parties do not always fit neatly into a left–right spectrum. However, we can identify which parties are generally left wing in their views, which are right wing and which are in the centre of the political spectrum. Parties which are not very left wing may be described as centre-left, and on the other side parties may be described as centre-right. Table 16 shows where UK parties fit into the left–right scheme. There are also notes about different tendencies within some parties.

Table 16 Parties and the left–right spectrum

Party	Left–right position	Notes
Conservative	Centre-right	There is a large right-wing minority in the party.
Labour	Left	The leadership group is left wing but many MPs are centre-left.
Liberal Democrat	Centre-left	The future is uncertain.
UKIP	Right	Now in serious decline
Green Party	Left	The party's main concern is environmentalism, but it has other left-wing views.
Scottish National Party	Centre-left	Independence is the main policy.
Plaid Cymru	Centre-left	

The funding of UK political parties

Parties are currently funded in a number of ways:

- collecting membership subscriptions from members
- holding fundraising events such as fetes, festivals, conferences and dinners
- receiving donations from supporters
- raising loans from wealthy individuals or banks
- the self-financing of candidates for office
- up to £2 million per party is available in grants from the electoral commission (see detail below), plus 'Short money' which grants funds to parties for research depending on their size

Short money Named after Ted Short, the politician who introduced it, Short money refers to funds given to opposition parties to facilitate their parliamentary work (research facilities etc.).The amount is based on how many seats and votes each party won at the previous election.

Why is party funding controversial?

1 The income of parties varies considerably, as shown in Table 17. This means that larger parties have a huge advantage over smaller parties.

Table 17 Income of parties reported in 2015 income of parties reported in 2015 (central funds)

Party	Income from all sources (£ millions)
Labour	51.2
Conservatives	41.9
Liberal Democrats	7.9
Scottish National Party	6.0
UK Independence Party	5.8
Green Party	3.0
Plaid Cymru	0.7

Source: Electoral Commission

2 Funding by large donors, both individuals and companies (party donations from abroad are illegal), may give those donors secretive and unaccountable influence.

3 Some party donations verge on being corrupt. In particular, some may be given in the hope and expectation that the donor be given an honour such as a peerage or a knighthood.

4 Because party memberships (and membership subscriptions) have been declining parties rely more heavily on donations from rich benefactors.

Exam tip

You do not need to know exactly what various parties receive, but try to remember a few rough statistics to illustrate the current inequality.

What measures have been proposed to solve these party funding problems?

1 Impose restrictions on the size of individual donations to parties. This is broadly the system used in the USA (though donors can grant funds to thousands of individual candidates). To be effective the cap would have to be relatively low.

2 Impose tight restrictions on how much parties are allowed to spend. This would make large-scale fundraising futile.

3 Restrict donations to individuals, i.e. outlawing donations from businesses, pressure groups and trade unions.

4 Replace all funding with state grants for parties, paid for out of general taxation.

You need to consider the arguments for and against the idea of the state funding political parties in order to remove some of the problems described above. Table 18 summarises the arguments on either side.

Table 18 Should UK parties receive state funding?

Arguments for	Arguments against
It will end the opportunities for the corrupt use of donations (often known as 'cash for honours').	Taxpayers may object to funding what can be considered to be 'private' organisations.
It will end the possibilities of 'hidden' forms of influence through funding.	It will be difficult to know how to distribute funding. Should it be on the basis of past performance (in which case large parties will retain their advantage) or on the basis of future aspirations (which is vague)?
It will reduce the huge financial advantage that large parties enjoy and give smaller parties the opportunity to make progress.	Parties may lose some of their independence and will see themselves as organs of the state.
It will improve democracy by ensuring wider participation from groups who have no ready source of funds.	State funding may lead to excessive state regulation of parties.

Cash for honours The belief that some donors give to parties in order to receive an honour such as a peerage or knighthood.

Established political parties

The generally accepted three established parties are the Conservatives, Labour and the Liberal Democrats. The Liberal Democrats have been in decline, but their fortunes may well recover and they still have a large membership and many members in the House of Lords and in local government. Policies constantly change and it is vital to keep up with these developments. It is especially difficult to sum up Labour policies as the party has a serious internal split. The principal policies of the three parties as they were after the June 2017 general election are outlined below.

Conservatives

- To achieve a surplus government budget as soon after 2012 as possible.
- To renew the Trident nuclear submarine missile system.
- To negotiate the best possible terms of leaving the European Union.
- To increase the personal tax-free income tax allowance to £12,500 per annum.
- To reduce the tax burden on company profits.
- To reduce the tax burden on middle-income groups.
- Generous increases in the minimum wage by 2020.
- Not to increase the rate of VAT.
- To reduce tax avoidance and evasion by individuals and companies.
- To build a Northern Powerhouse by investing in infrastructure in Northern England.

Labour

(These are the policies of the leadership but not the majority of the parliamentary members.)

- To increase taxation on the wealthiest groups in society.
- To increase taxation on company profits.
- To reduce taxation on low-income groups.
- To attack tax evasion and avoidance.
- Significant increases in the minimum wage.
- To reverse welfare benefit cuts implemented since 2010.

Exam tip

You must be completely up to date with party policies even though these are constantly changing. Differentiate between solid, permanent policy positions and temporary changes in detail.

- To bring the railways, Royal Mail and water supply under public ownership.
- Large-scale government borrowing for capital spending on transport, schools and hospitals.
- To restore trade union powers removed since the 1980s.
- To increase spending on health and social care.
- To abolish university tuition fees.
- To introduce free nursery education for all children.

Liberal Democrats

- Strong measures to protect the environment and to promote renewable sources of energy.
- To reform the constitution to make it more democratic.
- Reduce taxes on low-income groups.
- Reduce the levels of tax avoidance and evasion.
- Significant increases in the minimum wage.
- Large increases in spending on health, social care and education.
- Restoration of the pre-2010 levels of some welfare benefits.

Knowledge check 5

Study the policies of the three main parties. Identify the following:
- a policy on which all three parties agree
- two policies on which Labour and the Conservatives disagree
- two policies stressed more by the Liberal Democrats than the other two parties

Factions within parties

The different factions *within* parties are almost as important as the differences *between* parties. All major parties contain important factions within them. These are summarised below.

Conservatives

- Thatcherism (New Right) — supports the policies adopted in the 1980s. They include neo-liberal ideas of free markets, low taxation, low levels of welfare benefits and the weakening of trade unions, plus neo-conservatism which wishes to see a strong, authoritarian state. The main group is called **Conservative Way Forward**.
- Liberal progressive conservatism — opposes the Thatcherite agenda and accepts the need for greater social justice, liberal policies towards lifestyles and a balanced view of welfare versus low taxation. The **Tory Reform Group** is the main example.
- One-nation Tories — now a small minority who wish to avoid policies which may be socially divisive.
- Eurosceptics — after the UK's decision to leave the EU, this group hopes that the UK will not remain in the European single market or the European customs union but will claim full economic independence.

Labour

There are two main groups:
- The supporters of Jeremy Corbyn, known as **Momentum**, support left-wing socialist policies such as the re-nationalisation of some important industries and

Neo-liberalism A belief that the state should interfere as little as possible in labour markets (wages and working conditions), financial markets (regulation of financial organisations) and product markets (regulation of competition between private enterprises). It is also a belief that welfare benefits should be minimised and taxes kept as low as possible.

One nation A term related to conservatism. One-nation conservatives support policies that will help to unite the nation and avoid social conflict.

strong regulation of public utilities, strengthening trade unions and raising taxes to redistribute income and improve welfare services. They are sometimes referred to as **Old Labour**.

■ The opponents of Corbyn and supporters of centrist policies such as poverty reduction programmes, mild redistribution of income, support for the welfare state but not excessively generous state benefits, who also take a pragmatic approach to economic management. Sometimes they are referred to as **New Labour** supporters or even **Blairites**.

Liberal Democrats

■ Most Liberal Democrats support centre-left policies similar to those adopted by the centrists in the Labour Party, together with a strong position on environmental control and constitutional reform. These are sometimes described as **modern liberals**.

■ So-called **Orange Book liberals** support constitutional reform and environmentalism, but also support neo-liberal policies which would establish very free product, labour and financial markets. This is a throwback to the nineteenth-century liberals who were known as **classical liberals**.

> **Knowledge check 6**
>
> Place these party factions into the left–centre–right spectrum:
> ■ Momentum
> ■ Tory Reform Group
> ■ Conservative Way Forward
> ■ Mainstream Liberal Democrats
> ■ Blairites

Emerging and minor political parties

Parties to be considered under this heading include:

■ Scottish National Party (SNP)
■ United Kingdom Independence Party (UKIP)
■ Plaid Cymru (Welsh nationalists)
■ Green Party
■ Democratic Unionist Party (Northern Ireland conservatives)
■ Sinn Fein (Northern Ireland Irish nationalists)

Table 19 shows the general political stance of minor parties on the left–right spectrum plus their main policies.

Table 19 The political stance of small parties in the UK

Party	Principal policy	General political stance
Scottish National Party	Scottish independence	Centre-left
UKIP	UK to leave the EU	Right
Green Party	Environmental protection	Left
Plaid Cymru	More self-government for Wales	Centre-left
Democratic Unionist Party (DUP)	Close links between Northern Ireland and the UK	Right
Sinn Fein	Reunification of Ireland	Centre-left

Old Labour A term commonly used to describe left-wing Labour policies which dominated the party in the 1940s and in the 1970s and 1980s.

New Labour A term commonly used to describe the moderate policies of the Labour Party that were dominant between the early 1990s and 2015.

Modern liberals A term which relates to liberals in recent history who accept that government interference can be justified in the interests of welfare and social justice.

Classical liberals This term refers to nineteenth-century liberals who believed that there should be minimum interference by government in society and the economy.

Northern Ireland parties are important in the context of Northern Ireland itself, but normally have relatively little impact on the politics of the UK as a whole, beyond occupying 18 seats in the House of Commons. They become more important when the government parliamentary majority is small and so may need their support to secure a majority for its policies.

The importance of other parties in the UK

Small parties have a number of impacts on UK politics:

■ When the governing party lacks an overall Commons majority, it may survive by reaching an agreement of support with a minor party. The Conservative Party made such a pact with the Democratic Unionist Party of Northern Ireland in 2017.
■ A party that wins large numbers of votes (though not necessarily seats) may influence large parties who fear losing votes to it. This is most true of UKIP and the Conservatives and the Green Party and Labour.
■ If an emerging party wins a significant number of seats in the House of Commons it can become influential as a member of the opposition. This has become true of the SNP since 2015 and the DUP after 2017.

The ideas and policies of minor parties

Table 20 summarises some of the key policies of five of the minor parties.

Table 20 Minor party policies

Party	Examples of policies
SNP	■ Scottish independence ■ Failing independence, greater autonomous powers for Scotland within the UK ■ Redistribution of income from rich to poor ■ Strong support for public sector health and education ■ Investment in renewable energy
UKIP	■ UK to leave the European single market ■ Strong controls over immigration ■ Preference for British citizens in jobs, housing, welfare and education ■ An attack on companies that avoid and evade tax
Plaid Cymru	■ Similar nationalist policies to the SNP, but acceptance that Welsh independence is unlikely for many years ■ Similar economic and social policies to the SNP
Green Party	■ Strong controls on environmental damage and strict emissions control targets ■ Very large investment in the generation of renewable energy ■ Radical redistribution of income from rich to poor ■ Radical constitutional reform
DUP	■ Strengthen ties with the UK ■ Improve Northern Ireland infrastructure ■ Resist socially progressive ideas such as same-sex marriage, legal abortion

Consensus and adversary politics

Consensus politics refers to the following circumstances:

■ A period when there is a great deal of political agreement between the main parties.

Nationalism Nationalism in the UK mainly means a desire for national independence — the SNP seeks independence for Scotland and Plaid Cymru hopes future support for Welsh independence will grow. UKIP wants independence from European influence, while Sinn Fein wishes to see a united Ireland.

Consensus This refers to widespread agreement on an issue or a general political stance. Consensus implies more than a narrow majority of support, but, rather, agreement across party lines.

- The parties disagree on the detail of policies rather than the basic principles.
- Such a period was 2010–15 when the policies of the coalition government were similar to those adopted by Labour under Ed Miliband.

Adversary politics refers to the following circumstances:

- There is a wide distinction between the policies of the main parties.
- The division is ideological in nature.
- Such a period was the 1980s when the Thatcherite policies were neo-liberal and neo-conservative, but Labour adopted left-wing policies.
- There was adversarial politics between the Conservative-led governments and the Corbyn-led Labour Party after 2015.

Exam tip

Do not confuse 'adversary politics' (as described above) and 'adversarial politics'. Adversarial politics refers to a *style* of politics which appears to be very aggressive (e.g. Prime Minister's Question Time) but does not necessarily reflect fundamental policy divisions.

UK political parties in context

Party systems and classifications

Party system refers to the number of parties that win significant representation and/or have significant influence in the political system. Different countries have different party systems. In the UK there are different party systems in different parts of the country. Table 21 shows the main descriptions of party systems and where they exist within the UK.

Party system A description of how many parties have a significant number of seats or a significant influence in a political system.

Table 21 Party systems in the UK

Type	Description	Where it operates
Dominant-party system	One party dominates the number of seats in the legislative body.	Scottish Parliament
Two-party system	Only two parties have significant representation.	English constituencies
Three-party system	Three parties have significant representation.	Since 2015 only three parties have had significant seats in the House of Commons: Conservative, Labour and the SNP
Multi-party system	Four or more parties have a significant number of representatives elected.	Northern Ireland and Welsh assemblies plus many local government areas

Exam tip

When discussing the significance of parties, do not forget parties which may not win many seats but which have an influence over other parties and the political agenda because they win many votes. This applied to UKIP over the EU referendum in 2016 and to the Green Party in a more general way.

Table 22 shows two-party dominance in the UK Parliament up to 1992 followed by something more like a three-party system and then a return to two-party dominance in 2017.

Table 22 Two-party dominance in the UK, 1987–2017

Election year	Conservative seats	Labour seats	Third party seats	% of seats won by the two main parties
1987	376	229	22	93.0
1992	336	271	20	93.2
1997	165	418	46	88.4
2001	166	413	52	87.8
2005	198	356	62	85.6
2010	307	258	57	86.9
2015	331	232	56	86.7
2017	318	262	35	89.2

Table 23 shows how the dominance of the two main parties *in terms of total votes cast* declined up to 2017 but then increased again in that year's June election.

Table 23 The decline in two-party dominance, 1979–2017

Election year	% votes won by the two main parties
1979	80.8
1983	70.0
1987	75.1
1992	77.5
1997	75,5
2001	72.4
2005	67.5
2010	65.1
2015	67.3
2017	82.4

Table 24 shows the seats won in the Scottish Parliament in 2016, demonstrating that it is a multi-party system:

Table 24 Elections to the Scottish Parliament, 2016

Party	Seats won
SNP	63
Conservatives	31
Labour	24
Green Party	6
Liberal Democrats	5

Factors in party success and failure

Much of the material relating to the success or otherwise of parties is contained in the section on 'Voting behaviour and the media' (see pages 39–47). At this stage we can identify the main factors as outlined below.

Knowledge check 7

Study the full results of the most recent general election in the UK. Which parties won over 1 million votes?

Valence

Valence refers to how people generally view the party's image. It includes such qualities as:

- How competent was the party in the past when it was last in office?
- How economically responsible does it appear to be?
- Is it trustworthy?

Quality of leadership

This includes the following qualities which are known to attract support:

- experience
- decisiveness
- ability to lead
- media image
- intelligence
- apparent honesty

Unity

Parties that are disunited tend to fare badly at elections. The opposite is true of united parties. Positive and negative examples include:

- In 1983 and 1987 a divided Labour Party was heavily defeated by a united Conservative Party under Margaret Thatcher.
- In 1997 the Conservatives were divided over Europe and lost heavily to Labour, which was united around Tony Blair's New Labour agenda.
- In 2015 the divided Liberal Democratic Party lost most of its seats in the UK Parliament.

The media

A party that is heavily criticised in the press finds it difficult to secure public confidence. This adversely affected the Labour Party in 1983 and 2010. However, the Labour Party did manage to overcome ferocious press opposition in the 2017 election campaign. It did this partly by mobilising social media in its favour.

The role of parties in the UK

Finally it is necessary to consider a general assessment of the role of parties in the UK system, in particular the extent to which they play a negative or positive role in the political system. Table 25 summarises the role of parties in the UK system.

Table 25 The role of parties in the UK's representative democracy

Positive aspects	Negative aspects
They provide open opportunities for people to become active in politics. They are inclusive and make few demands on members.	Adversarial party politics is negative in that it denies the creation of consensus and reduces issues to false, simplistic choices.
They make political issues coherent and help to make government accountable.	Parties claim legitimacy through their electoral mandate even when they are elected to power with a minority of the popular vote.
They help to make elections and the operation of parliament effective and understandable to the public.	Parties sometimes become over-elitist so that small leadership groups can dominate policy making to the detriment of internal democracy.

Valence The general image a party portrays, which affects the level of electoral support it can achieve.

Summary

When you have completed this topic you should have a thorough knowledge of the following information and issues:

■ the features and functions of political parties
■ the meaning and importance of the doctrine of mandate and manifesto
■ the nature of left- and right-wing politics
■ the reasons why party funding is controversial
■ the proposed solutions to the funding problem
■ the arguments for and against state funding of parties
■ the principal policies of the three main parties
■ the significant factions within the main parties
■ the nature and importance of small and emerging parties
■ the classification of party systems
■ the significance of party systems in the UK
■ an assessment of whether parties play a positive or negative role in the UK political system

In addition, you should have gathered appropriate information to help you answer the following wide-ranging questions:

1 Assess the importance of political parties in the UK political system.
2 Are the policy differences within parties as significant as the differences between them?
3 Assess the impact of smaller parties in the UK political system.
4 To what extent is the UK still a two-party system?
5 To what extent do policies or other factors determine how well parties perform at elections?

Electoral systems

Different electoral systems explained and assessed

First past the post

The main features of the first-past-the-post **electoral system** are these:

- The country is divided into constituencies.
- Each constituency returns one Member of Parliament (MP).
- At elections each party presents one candidate for election.
- The winner of the election is the candidate who wins more votes than any other candidate. This is known as a *plurality*.
- It is not necessary to win an overall (over 50%) majority to win a seat. About half the winning candidates in the UK do not win over 50% of the votes in their constituency.

> **Exam tip**
>
> When preparing for exams, it is vital that you can describe the workings of all the electoral systems included in the specification clearly and succinctly. This will save you time for answering the rest of the questions.

Safe and marginal seats

One of the key issues concerning first past the post is that it tends to produce a large number of seats which are 'safe' seats. A **safe seat** can be defined as a seat where only one party is realistically expected to win. Put another way, it is a seat that rarely, if ever, changes hands between parties from one election to the next. A **marginal seat** is one where the normal result is close between two or more parties so it is uncertain which party will win at each election. This feature causes problems:

- Safe seats mean that the voters are effectively disenfranchised — whichever way they vote, it will make no difference to the inevitable result.
- Votes in safe seats are therefore 'wasted' votes.
- This means also that votes are of unequal value. Votes in marginal seats are more valuable than votes in safe seats because they are liable to affect the result.
- Parties tend to put most of their attention into marginal seats at elections so safe seats tend to be ignored.
- When governments make decisions with local considerations they will look at marginal seats more favourably. Safe seats get less favourable treatment.

Electoral system A system for converting votes into seats gained in a legislature.

Safe seat A constituency where the result at elections is not in doubt because one party invariably wins it.

Marginal seat A constituency where the result of an election is usually in doubt. Elections are normally closely contested.

The advantages and disadvantages of the first-past-the-post system are shown in Table 26.

Table 26 An assessment of first past the post

Advantages	Disadvantages
It is easy to understand and produces a clear result in each constituency. The result is also known very quickly.	The overall outcome is not proportional or fair. Some parties win more seats than their support warrants, while others win less than they deserve.
It produces one single representative for each constituency and so creates a close constituency–MP bond.	It means that many votes are effectively wasted because they can have no impact on the outcome in safe seats. Many seats become part of party 'heartlands', where there is no possibility of a realistic challenge from other parties. It also produces 'electoral deserts', where there is effectively no party competition.
Accountability of the individual MP is clear to the electors.	Votes are of unequal value in that votes in safe seats are less valuable than votes in marginal seats. UKIP votes were of hugely less value than Conservative votes in 2015.
The system tends to produce a clear winner in the general election, i.e. a single party with a parliamentary majority. This helps to promote strong, stable, decisive government.	It encourages some voters to vote tactically and so abandon the party they really want to support.
It helps to prevent small parties breaking into the system. This is useful if the small parties are undesirable 'extremists'.	It prevents new parties breaking into the system and so produces political 'inertia'.
Arguably first past the post has stood the test of time. Abandoning the system would be a dangerous step into the unknown.	It has, since 1945, always resulted in the winning party securing much less than half the popular vote. In 2015 the winning Conservative Party was elected with just 36.9% of the popular vote; 63.1% of voters voted against the governing party. In 2005 Labour won the election with a majority of 66 from only 35.2% of the popular vote. This calls into question the legitimacy of the government.
	First past the post always used to deliver governments with a majority of the seats in the House of Commons. In 2010 it failed to do this. In 2015 the Conservative Party only secured a fragile 12-seat majority and in 2017 another hung parliament resulted. It could be argued that if the system fails to deliver a decisive result, it cannot be defended in the future.

The additional member system (AMS)

This system operates in elections to the Scottish Parliament and the Welsh Assembly. It works like this:

- Two-thirds of the seats are elected using first past the post, as for UK general elections.
- The other third of the seats are elected on the basis of closed regional list voting. The country is divided into regions and each party offers a list of candidates for

each region. Voters have two votes — one for the constituency and the other for one of the party lists. Seats are awarded to each party in the list system in proportion to the votes cast — the more votes, the more seats awarded.

■ There is an important variation in the regional list part of the vote. The variable **top-up system** adjusts the proportions of votes cast on the list system. This is a complex calculation, but, in essence, what happens is the seats awarded from the list system are adjusted to give a more proportional result. It is known as the **D'Hondt** method.

■ Parties that do less well in the constituencies (typically Conservatives or Greens) have their proportion of list votes adjusted upwards. Those that do proportionally well under first past the post (typically Labour) have their list votes adjusted downwards.

■ The overall effect of variable top-up is to make the total result close to proportional of the total votes cast in both systems.

An assessment of the additional member system is shown in Table 27.

Table 27 The additional member system (AMS)

Advantages	Drawbacks
It produces a broadly proportional outcome and so is fair to all parties.	It produces two classes of representative — those with a constituency and those elected through the lists. The latter tend to be senior.
It gives voters two votes and so more choice.	It is more complex than first past the post. Having two votes can confuse some voters.
It combines preserving constituency representation with a proportional outcome.	It can result in the election of extremist candidates.
	It is more likely to result in minority or coalition government.

Single transferable vote (STV)

The STV system operates in this way:

■ There are six seats available in each constituency.

■ Each party is permitted to put up as many candidates as there are seats, i.e. up to six. In practice parties do not adopt six candidates as they have no chance of winning all six seats available. Four is the normal maximum number from each party.

■ Voters place the candidates in their order of preference by putting a number 1, 2, 3 etc. beside their names.

■ Voters can vote for candidates from different parties or even all the parties, though few actually do.

■ At the count an **electoral quota** is calculated. This is established by taking the total number of votes cast, dividing it by the number of seats available plus 1. So, if 50,000 votes were cast and six seats are available, the quota is $50,000 \div (6 + 1 = 7)$. This works out as 7,143. One is then added, giving a final figure of 7,144.

■ At first all the first preferences are counted for each candidate. Any candidates who achieve the quota are elected automatically.

Top-up system Part of the additional member system requires that parties which are unfairly represented by the first-past-the-post part of the system will have their seats 'topped up' preferentially to make the overall result more proportional to total votes cast.

Electoral quota A feature of the single transferable vote system, the quota (known as a Droop quota) calculates the number of votes a candidate must achieve to be elected. It is calculated by the total votes, divided by seats available plus one.

- After this stage the counting is complex. Essentially the second and subsequent preferences from the ballot papers of the elected candidates are added to the other candidates. If this results in an individual achieving the quota, he or she is elected.
- This process continues until six candidates have achieved the quota and are elected.

An assessment of STV is shown in Table 28.

Table 28 The single transferable vote system

Advantages	Drawbacks
It produces a broadly proportional outcome.	It is quite a complex system that some voters do not understand.
It gives voters a very wide choice of candidates to choose from. The second and subsequent choices of the voters are taken into consideration in the counting.	The vote counting is complicated and can take a long time.
Voters can vote for candidates from different parties and show a preference between candidates of the same party.	It can help candidates with extremist views to be elected.
As there are six representatives per constituency, each voter has a choice of those to represent them and usually can be represented by someone from the party they support.	With six representatives per constituency the lines of accountability are not clear.
	It is more likely to result in **minority** or **coalition government**.

Supplementary vote (SV)

This system is used to elect a single candidate, such as a mayor, and is designed to ensure that the winner has a majority of support from the electors. It operates like this:

- Voters have two choices, a first and second choice. If any candidate achieves an overall majority, i.e. 50%+, of the first choice or round, he or she is automatically elected.
- If this does not happen the top two candidates go into a second round of counting. All the others drop out.
- The second choice votes are added to the first choices to give two final totals. As there are only two candidates left, one of them must achieve an absolute majority.
- Therefore the winner has an overall majority of a combination of first- and second-choice votes.

An assessment of SV is shown in Table 29.

Table 29 The supplementary vote system

Advantages	Drawbacks
The winning candidate can claim to have an overall majority of support.	A winning candidate may not enjoy the first choice support of an overall majority.
It is relatively simple for voters to understand.	The winning candidate may win on second choices.
Voters' first and second choices are relevant.	

Minority government
When no party wins an overall majority in the House of Commons it may form a minority government. This is a common form of government in Scotland and Wales. Such governments tend to be weak and unstable because of their lack of majority support.

Coalition government
When no party wins an overall majority in the House of Commons two or more parties may form a coalition government, as occurred in the UK in 2010–15. The coalition parties share seats in government and agree policies between them.

Knowledge check 8

Study the four electoral systems described above. Which system:

- Is likely to produce the most proportional result?
- Gives most choice to voters?
- Is most likely to produce an overall majority for the winning party?

Table 30 summarises the electoral systems used in the UK. It also shows the distinctions between plurality, hybrid, proportional and majority systems.

Table 30 Summary of electoral systems used in the UK

System	Type of system	Where used
First past the post	Plurality	UK general elections English and Welsh local government elections
Additional member system	Hybrid	Scottish parliamentary elections Welsh Assembly elections Greater London Assembly elections
STV	Proportional	All Northern Ireland elections Local elections in Scotland
Supplementary vote	Majority	To elect city mayors

Exam tip

Remember that the term 'proportional representation' does not refer to a *particular* electoral system. It is a way of describing several systems that produce a proportional outcome such as STV.

Comparing first past the post with other systems

Such comparisons should be considered in the light of what one hopes to achieve through the electoral system. Table 31 shows a variety of objectives and suggests which electoral system is most likely to achieve each objective.

Table 31 Comparing electoral systems on the basis of objectives

Objective	Most appropriate system
Strong, stable government	First past the post
Maximum voter choice	Single transferable vote
A multi-party system	Single transferable vote
Strong constituency representation	First past the post
A proportional outcome	Additional member system
An absolute majority for the winner	Supplementary vote
Votes are of equal value	Single transferable vote

Proportionality The quality of an electoral system measuring the extent to which the result, in terms of seats won by each party, is proportional to the votes cast for each party.

The case for retaining or replacing first past the post

The advantages and disadvantages of **first past the post** are shown in Table 26 above. In addition to that evaluation there are a number of further arguments for retention or replacement.

Arguments for **retention** include:

- It is a tried and tested system with widespread public support.
- It retains a strong MP–constituency link.
- It does normally tend to produce strong governments with a working majority in the House of Commons, although this is now a dubious argument after three elections which failed to produce a decisive majority (2010, 2015 and 2017).
- Replacing it will exchange the known for the unknown, with unquantifiable consequences.

First past the post The name given to the electoral system used for UK general elections.

Arguments for **replacement** include:

- The 2010, 2015 and 2017 elections suggest it no longer guarantees a strong, decisive government.
- It produces a very unrepresentative outcome.
- Proportional representation means that voters are better served because every vote counts.
- Replacement will eliminate the problem of too many safe seats.

Referendums

The experience of referendums in the UK since 1997

The use of referendums to settle important political issues, normally constitutional matters, has become increasingly popular since 1997. Table 32 summarises the use of referendums since 1997.

Table 32 Referendums in the UK since 1997

Year	Issue	Level	Why held	Yes (%)	No (%)	Turnout (%)
1997	Should additional powers be devolved to Scotland and a Scottish Parliament established?	Scotland	A fundamental change in the system of government needed popular consent.	74.3	25.7	60.4
1997	Should additional powers be devolved to Wales and a Welsh Assembly established?	Wales	A fundamental change in the system of government needed popular consent.	50.3	49.7	50.1
1998	Should the Belfast Agreement be implemented?	Northern Ireland	This required support across the whole divided community.	71.7	28.9	81.0
2004	Should additional powers be devolved to northeast England and a regional assembly established?	Northeast England	A fundamental change in the system of government needed popular consent.	22.1	77.9	47.7
2005	Should a 'congestion charge' zone be introduced in Edinburgh?	Edinburgh	It was a highly controversial proposal.	25.6	74.4	61.7
2011	Should the UK adopt the alternative vote system for general elections?	National	The coalition government was divided on the issue of electoral reform.	32.1	67.9	42.2
2014	Should Scotland become a completely independent country?	Scotland	A fundamental question about who governs Scotland.	44.7	55.3	84.6
2016	Should the UK remain a member of the EU?	National	A fundamental constitutional question. The governing Conservative Party was split on the issue. Also to meet the challenge of UKIP.	48.1	51.9	72.2

Knowledge check 9

Study the outcomes of referendums since 1997. Identify:

- Which referendum had the highest turnout?
- Which referendums were locally based?
- Which referendums were regionally based?
- Which referendum had the highest majority?
- Which referendum had the narrowest majority?

The reasons why referendums have been held

The main reasons why referendums have been used to settle political issues, rather than using government and parliament, include the following:

- An issue might be very divisive so a referendum can settle the issue and unite the population. **Example: the devolution referendums of 1997.**
- An issue may be of huge constitutional significance and so requires pure democracy. **Example: the 2014 referendum on Scottish independence.**
- It helps to entrench and safeguard constitutional changes. **Example: the referendum on the Good Friday Agreement in Northern Ireland, 1998.**
- To judge public opinion on an issue. **Example: local referendums on congestion charges.**

The case for and against referendums

Referendums have become the subject of controversy, especially after the EU referendum of 2016 proved to be so divisive. This was partly because the result was so close and partly because it revealed how divided the UK was on the issue of the European Union. Furthermore it presented a binary choice — remain or leave — when many said the issue was more complex than that. The 2016 referendum is the best example to use when discussing the problems of referendum use. Other referendums, however, have proved to be more successful. The arguments concerning referendums are summarised in Table 33.

Binary choice This means there are only two possible outcomes — yes or no. All referendums are binary even if the issue could have more complicated responses.

Exam tip

When assessing the use of referendums, consider that the alternatives to referendums are votes in parliament or decisions by executive government. You should try to evaluate which of the three bodies — the people, parliament and government — is best suited to resolving an issue.

Table 33 Evaluating the use of referendums in the UK

Arguments for	Arguments against
Referendums are the purest form of democracy, uncorrupted by the filter of representative democracy. They demonstrate the pure will of the people, as occurred in the EU vote.	The people may not be able to understand the complexities of an issue such as the consequences of leaving the EU or adopting a new electoral system.
Referendums can mend rifts in society, as occurred with the decisive result of the 1998 vote on the Belfast Agreement.	Referendums can also cause social rifts. This arguably occurred in both 2014 in Scotland and in 2016 in the EU referendum.
Referendums can solve conflicts *within* the political system and so stave off a crisis. This was especially the case with the EU referendums in both 1975 and 2016.	There is a danger that the excessive use of referendums may undermine the authority of representative democracy. This has been a particular danger in some states in the USA.
Referendums are particularly useful when the *expressed* (as opposed to *implied*) consent of the people is important, so that the decision will be respected. This was very true of the votes on devolution in 1997.	A referendum can represent the 'tyranny of the majority'. This means that the majority that wins the vote can use their victory to force the minority to accept a change which is against their interests. The Scots, who voted strongly to stay in the EU in 2016 claimed they were being tyrannised by the English majority.
Arguably the people are much more informed than they have ever been in the past. The internet and social media in particular have facilitated this. This makes them more capable of making decisions for themselves rather than relying on elected representatives.	Voters may be swayed by emotional rather than rational appeals. It may also be that they are influenced by false information.
	Some questions should not be reduced to a simple yes/no answer; they are more complicated. Certainly the 2011 question on electoral reform is an example of this. Perhaps several *different* options should have been considered, not just one.

Electoral systems analysis

Debates about the use of different electoral systems in the UK

Before considering the issue of what electoral system is appropriate for which desired outcome, we should consider the positive and negative aspects of elections in the UK. These can be summarised as outlined below.

Positive features of UK elections

- There is relatively little corruption. Some electoral fraud takes place in some areas but it is rare and usually detected. The secrecy of the ballot is virtually guaranteed. The counting of votes is carefully and thoroughly regulated. The conduct of elections is safeguarded by the Electoral Commission, which is independent of government.
- The constituency system ensures clear representation for citizens.
- Elections are held on a regular basis. This is normally every 5 years, except under unusual circumstances.
- UK elections are free in that it is relatively easy and cheap for any citizen to stand for election and virtually all adults are permitted to vote.

Negative features of UK elections

- The first-past-the-post system used for general elections and local elections in England and Wales is widely acknowledged to be unfair and certainly unrepresentative. This means that many votes are wasted and votes are of unequal value.
- Small parties find it very difficult to gain a foothold because of the electoral system in England.
- UK general elections produce governments that do not enjoy a majority of the support of the electorate. In recent elections the winning party has failed to achieve 40% of the popular vote.

The impact of electoral systems on types of government, voter choice, fairness and proportionality

Table 34 summarises the different outcomes and qualities of first past the post (FPTP) in comparison with two other systems. In each case there is an evaluation in terms of the party system, government formation, voter choice, fairness and proportionality.

Table 34 Three electoral systems compared

System	Party system	Government formation	Voter choice	Fairness	Proportionality
FPTP	Tends to two parties	Strong government with a majority normally	Little choice	Votes are of unequal value with many wasted	Very disproportionate result
AMS	Multi-party	Difficult for one party to gain a majority	Voters have two votes	There are fewer wasted votes	Outcome is very proportional
STV	Multi-party	A majority government is very unlikely	Voters have many choices	Extremely fair to voters and candidate	Very proportional outcomes

Summary

When you have completed this topic you should have a thorough knowledge of the following information and issues:

- how the first-past-the-post electoral system works
- how various alternative electoral systems work
- what is the impact of various electoral systems
- the case for introducing proportional representation for general elections
- the case for retaining first past the post for general elections in the UK
- what referendums have been used in the UK since 1997
- the reasons why referendums have been used
- the arguments for and against the use of referendums
- how to compare different electoral systems

In addition, you should have gathered appropriate information to help you answer the following wide-ranging questions:

1 Assess the arguments for the introduction of proportional representation for UK general elections.
2 Using examples, explain the relationship between electoral systems and party systems.
3 Explain the main circumstances under which referendums have been used in the UK.
4 Assess the case for the continued use of referendums to settle political and constitutional issues in the UK.
5 Make a case for retaining first past the post as the electoral system for general elections in the UK.

■ Voting behaviour and the media

Class voting and other social factors in voting patterns

Class and voting

You need to know in general what the various classes are. Broadly speaking they look like this:

- **Class AB**   Higher managerial, company director, higher professional such as lawyers
- **Class C1**   Supervisors, clerical workers, junior managers, lower professional such as nurses
- **Class C2**   Skilled manual occupations
- **Class DE**   Unskilled manual workers, basic catering, unemployed

The link between people's **social class** and the party they are most likely to support has declined. It used to be the case that the vast majority of class AB voted Conservative, but the majority of class DE voted Labour. Tables 35 and 36 show how the link between social class and voting habits has changed since the 1960s.

Table 35 Class AB voting for the Conservatives

Election year	% class AB voting Conservative
1964	78
1987	57
1997	59
2010	40
2015	45
2017	43

Source: Ipsos MORI/ Earlham Sociology

Table 36 Class DE voting for Labour

Election year	% class DE voting Labour
1964	64
1987	53
1997	59
2010	40
2015	41
2017	59

Source: Ipsos MORI/ Earlham Sociology

Why has class-based voting declined? There are a number of reasons why this has occurred. They include:

- **Class dealignment**. A diminishing proportion of the population consider themselves a member of a specific class. Class is less important in society than it used to be.

Social class How we divide society up according to a person's occupation, though not income.

Class dealignment The increasing tendency for voters to support a particular party, not because of which class they come from, but according to an objective judgement of the quality of the parties. In other words, class has become a weaker indicator of which way a person will vote.

- The parties have tended to move towards the centre of the political spectrum which means they appeal to people across the class boundaries.
- Other factors than class have become important. Increasingly, voters have become unpredictable in their voting and are more influenced by the image of the parties than which class they seem to favour.

Partisanship and voting attachment

The main factor in **partisanship** today is a trend known as **partisan dealignment**. This means that a progressively smaller proportion of voters feel a strong attachment to one of the major parties. This decline in partisanship has a number of causes:

- Class dealignment has occurred (see above). This means that the old strong links between the working class and Labour and the middle class and the Conservatives have weakened (see Tables 35 and 36 above). As a result of class dealignment people have weaker party attachments.
- The parties have tended to adopt centrist policies which can attract a wider range of voter support.
- There is a growing support for smaller parties such as the Green Party and Scottish Nationalists.
- There is a general widespread dissatisfaction with the performance of parties at Westminster (demonstrated by UKIP voting and low turnouts up to 2017) so people feel less attachment to them. Nevertheless there was something of a revival in support for the two main parties in 2017.
- There has been a long-term decline in party membership, with the exception of a revival in Labour membership and activism in 2016–17, so there are fewer committed party supporters.

Despite these trends, class remains a fairly good predictor of how an individual will vote. Other social factors are also important and these are discussed below.

> **Knowledge check 10**
>
> Look at Tables 35 and 36. Answer the following questions:
> - What proportion of middle-class voters supported the Conservatives in (a) 1964 and (b) 2017?
> - What proportion of working-class voters supported the Labour Party in (a) 1964 and (b) 2017?
> - Which party appears to have suffered more from class dealignment since 1964?

Gender, age, ethnicity and region in voting patterns

The evidence is that gender is not a significant factor in voting behaviour. There is no significant difference between the support given by men and women to the three main UK parties. Furthermore this result has not changed over time. However, there is a strong correlation between the age of voters and the way they typically vote. Table 37 demonstrates the correlations:

Partisanship The extent to which people feel a strong and permanent attachment to one party, meaning they will always support that party at elections.

Partisan dealignment A widespread tendency for people to feel a weaker attachment to a particular party. This means a larger proportion of voters are willing to change their party allegiance between elections.

Table 37 Age and voting in four general elections

Age range	1979 % Con	1979 % Lab	1979 % All*	1997 % Con	1997 % Lab	1997 % LD*	2010 % Con	2010 % Lab	2010 % LD*	2015 % Con	2015 % Lab	2015 % LD*	2017 % Con	2017 % Lab	2017 % LD*
18–24	42	41	12	27	49	16	30	31	30	27	43	5	18	67	7
25–34	43	38	15	28	49	16	30	29	29	33	36	7	22	58	9
35–44**	46	35	16	28	48	17	31	26	26	35	35	10	30	50	9
45–54				31	41	20	28	26	26	36	33	8	40	39	9
55–64***	47	38	13	36	39	17	28	23	23	37	31	9	47	33	9
65+				36	41	17	44	31	16	47	23	8	59	23	10
Total, all ages	45	38	14	31	43	17	36	29	23	37	30	8	42	40	7

Source: IpsosMORI/Ashcroft polling

* The third party was the SDP/Liberal Alliance in 1979, the Liberal Democrats thereafter.

** In 1979 this figure is for 35–54.

***In 1979 this figure is for 55+.

The conclusions we can reach from these data about age and voting are as follows:

- The 18–24 age group is much more likely to support the Labour Party than the Conservatives.
- The 35–44 age group is the most likely range to support the Liberal Democrats.
- The older a voter is, the more likely they are to support the Conservative Party.

It is also true that the younger a voter is, the more likely they are to vote for a radical party. Up to 2017 this meant the Green Party or the Scottish National Party (see Table 38). However, young radicals switched to supporting Labour in large numbers in 2017.

Table 38 Voting by age for the Green Party and the SNP, 2017 general election

Age range	% Green Party	% Scottish National Party*
18–24	4	7
25–34	4	6
35–44	5	4
45–54	4	3
55–64	4	3
65+	2	3
Total, all ages	2	5

Source: IpsosMORI, YouGov

*Percentage relates to proportion of votes in the UK as a whole.

Turning to ethnicity there is an even more striking correlation. Table 39 indicates clearly that members of the black and minority ethnic (BME) community are far more likely to support Labour than the Conservatives although this bias is reducing gradually.

Table 39 Ethnicity and voting

Election	% BME voting Conservative	% BME voting Labour	% BME voting Liberal Democrat
1997	18	70	9
2010	16	60	20
2015	23	65	4
2017	21	65	6

Source: IpsosMORI

This is partly a class effect in that the BME community is more likely to be filling lower-paid occupations, but it is also to do with Labour's past record on securing equality for such groups and outlawing discrimination.

Knowledge check 11

Look at Tables 37, 38 and 39. Answer the following questions:

- What proportion of the 18–24 age group voted for the Green Party in 2017?
- Among the 65+ age group, what was the difference between their support for the Conservatives and Labour in 2017?
- What proportion of the 18–24 age group supported the Conservatives in 2017 compared to 1979?
- What proportion of the BME community supported Labour compared to the Conservatives in 2017?

There are wide disparities in regional voting in the UK. Indeed regional voting figures demonstrate that the UK is a very divided country as far as political allegiances are concerned. When looking at regional statistics, it is important to consider that class is a factor. It is clear that parts of the UK, especially the south of England, are largely middle class, while much of the north is working-class dominated. However, the regional variations cannot be accounted for solely by class. Table 40 shows the results of the 2017 general election broken down by region.

Table 40 2017 general election, voting by region (% seats)

Region	% Conservative	% Labour	% Liberal Democrat	SNP or Plaid Cymru
North of England	37.2	52.9	5.0	n/a
South of England	45.7	25.5	9.9	n/a
Midlands of England	49.7	41.6	4.4	n/a
London	34.9	43.7	7.7	n/a
Scotland	14.9	24.3	7.5	36.9
Wales	27.2	36.9	6.5	10.4

A number of conclusions can be drawn:

- The south of England is heavily dominated by the Conservative Party.
- The same is true of the Midlands, though to a slightly lesser extent.
- The north of England is Labour dominated.
- Scotland is heavily dominated by the SNP.
- London is different from the rest of the south of England in that Labour has more support there.

Table 41 summarises the relationships between a variety of social factors and voting for the parties.

Table 41 The influence of social and democratic factors

Factor	Estimated influence
Gender	There is virtually no difference in voting habits between men and women. There is a slight tendency for women to favour Labour.
Age	This is a key factor. Older voters favour the Conservatives (and UKIP) very significantly. Young voters have a Labour bias and also tend to support the Green Party.
Ethnicity	Another significant factor, although there are signs that it is weakening as a factor. A further trend is for more established immigrant groups to move towards favouring the Conservative Party.
Class	Class used to be the most important determinant of voting behaviour but is becoming much less influential. It does, however, remain significant.
Region	There are considerable variations in regional voting patterns. Scotland is heavily SNP dominated, while the south of England is solidly Conservative. The north of England is Labour country, while the English Midlands are closely contested between the two main parties.

Exam tip

In answers about what determines voting behaviour, it is important to distinguish between the long-term social factors described here and the short-term factors that influence each individual election such as valance, leadership, campaigns and press influence.

Floating voters

Floating voters are people who tend to change their voting behaviour at each election, in other words they are 'floating' between support for different parties. They are key voters as they determine the outcome of elections. Floating voters are more likely to take notice of party policies and the way in which parties campaign. The trends and influences described below relate mostly to this kind of voter.

Knowledge check 12

From the statistics shown in this section:
- Which is the *least* significant social factor?
- Which is the *most* significant social factor?

Voting trends and theories
Valence

Valence is one of the key factors in voting behaviour. It stands in opposition to **positional voting** where voters look at specific policies or groups of policies when making decisions about whom to vote for. Valence refers to the image of a party that voters typically have in their heads. In other words, it is about how much they respect

Positional voting This refers to voters making a choice of party based on its policies or on groups of policies such as the economy, the environment or immigration.

and trust a party rather than just what policies it is proposing. There are a number of features in valence:

- **Governing competence**. Does the party appear to be decisive? Did it govern well when it was last in power? It refers to such qualities as strength, decisiveness and sensitivity to public opinion. This was a problem for the Conservatives in 1997 and for Labour in 2010.
- **Economic competence.** How well did the party manage the economy last time it was in power? Do its current leaders and their policies inspire trust and suggest reliability? Labour lost confidence on economic management after the financial crash of 2008.
- **How united is the party?** Voters trust united parties but not disunited ones. The Conservative Party lost elections in 2001 and 2005 partly because it was divided within itself, largely over Europe.
- **Are the leaders admired and trusted?** The Liberal Democrats did well in 2010 because leader Nick Clegg was liked and respected. He lost respect after that and was heavily defeated in 2015. Ed Miliband, Labour's leader from 2010 to 2015, was not well respected and was a major cause of Labour's defeat in 2015.

Rational choice

As opposed to valence, the **rational choice model** refers to voters who make rational decisions about which party has the 'best' policies. Researchers always identify **salient issues** at each election. These are the issues that voters feel are most important. Some voters will base their choice on which parties respond best to these salient issues. Ipsos Mori polling research in 2015 put these four issues as the most salient in order of voter importance:

1 The state of the economy
2 Asylum and immigration
3 The NHS and healthcare
4 Education

The Conservative Party scored higher in voter opinions on issues 1 and 2 and Labour on issues 3 and 4. The outcome of the election reflected that correlation.

Issue voting

Issue voting is similar to rational choice, but here voters are concentrating on one single issue or a group of related issues. The choice of voters is often divided into two types:

- **Instrumental voting.** This is what voters think will be best *in their own interests*, for example which party will reduce my taxes? Which party will pay me most benefits? Which party is most likely to give me job security?
- **Expressive voting.** When voters think not of themselves but of the good of the whole community, for example, which party has the best environmental policies or law and order position or foreign policy?

Both are rational because they compare the pros and cons of supporting a particular party. Issue voting may be influenced by the contents of party manifestos, though few voters read them thoroughly. Manifestos are influential as a *general* guide to issues, rather than a specific analysis. They often show the *image* of the party as much as its policies.

Governing competence The image that voters have of a party based on how well it governed when last in power and how well they expect it to govern in the future.

Rational choice model Many voters who are not committed to any particular party or ideology make a rational choice between the parties when voting, weighing up the strengths and weaknesses of each. These voters are of particular importance to parties during election campaigning.

Salient issues Those policy issues at an election that voters consider the most important when making their party choice.

Economic influences

At most elections, the state of the economy and the economic policies of the parties are usually the most salient. To some extent the state of the economy may not be in the control of the government, but many voters will still blame the governing party if the economy is in a bad state and reward it if the economy is doing well. This means that the state of the economy, whether or not it is in the control of UK politicians, will affect party fortunes. Labour suffered such a fate in 2010 following the financial crisis and recession, but benefited from a strong economy in 2001 and 2005.

Party leaders and voting behaviour

The quality of the party leaders is an issue which stands alone in voting behaviour. The typical qualities that voters like to support are listed below. In each case a good example of the reputation of a leader is given:

- his or her record in office (e.g. Margaret Thatcher, 1979–87)
- compassion (e.g. John Major, 1990–92)
- decisiveness (e.g. Tony Blair, 1997–2001)
- strong leadership (e.g. Margaret Thatcher)
- clear vision (e.g. Tony Blair, Nicola Sturgeon for the SNP and Jeremy Corbyn in 2017)
- communication skills (e.g. David Cameron, 2010–16)
- populist appeal (e.g. Nigel Farage, 2015 and Jeremy Corbyn, 2017)

Examples of negative qualities perceived by voters, resulting in defeat, include:

- John Major's perceived weakness in the face of a divided party contributed to his heavy defeat in 1997.
- Gordon Brown was seen as weak and indecisive when he sought election in 2010.
- Nick Clegg was seen as untrustworthy when the Liberal Democrats suffered a crushing loss of seats in 2015.

Knowledge check 13

Study the impact of valence, salience, party image, leadership qualities etc. discussed above. Which factors contributed to the following election results?

- The heavy Conservative defeat in 1997
- The Conservative/Liberal Democrat victory in 2010
- The Conservative victory in 2015

Table 42 summarises the various non-social factors that affect voting behaviour.

Table 42 Non-social factors in voting behaviour

Factor type	Description
Valence	What is the general image of the party (e.g. trustworthiness, competence, unity)?
Rational choice	Which party has the best policies either for the individual voter or for the community as a whole?
Issue voting	Which single issue or group of issues attracts some voters?
Economic factors	What is the current state of the economy?
Leadership issues	Which leader is perceived to have the best qualities?

Exam tip

When discussing voting behaviour, always add some clear examples of how each factor has affected actual results in the past.

Voter turnout

The overall **turnout** in elections does not *in itself* affect the outcome of elections. However, the *different rates* of turnout among various social groups are influential. Some key features of turnout among various social groups include:

- Young voters turn out in smaller numbers than older voters. As Labour, Liberal Democrats and the Greens are more popular among the young, this means that these three parties are disadvantaged by this factor. This effect was reduced somewhat in 2017 when the votes of the 18–24 age group increased significantly.
- The over 65s turn out to vote in much larger numbers than other age groups (sometimes as high as 80%). As older people tend to support the Conservatives and UKIP, the two parties gain from higher turnout.
- Members of class DE vote in smaller numbers than class AB. This gives an advantage to the Conservative Party.
- Although Labour is supported by a large majority of BME (black and minority ethnic) voters, turnout in this group is relatively low.

Turnout The proportion of the total electorate who actually turn out to vote at an election or in a referendum.

The influence of the media

The broadcasting media in the UK are controlled to ensure that they have no political bias. They have, therefore, no discernible influence on electoral outcomes. The press, however, is a different matter. Newspapers in the UK virtually all have a political bias so they may have an influence.

The role and impact of the media on elections

Table 43 shows the political stance of UK newspapers.

Table 43 The political affiliations of the main UK newspapers at the 2017 election

Newspaper	Political preference	Circulation (000s)
Sun	Very strongly Conservative	1,667
Daily Mail	Very strongly Conservative	1,514
Daily Mirror	Very strongly Labour	725
Daily Telegraph	Very strongly Conservative	472
The Times	Moderate Conservative	451
Daily Star	No preference	443
Daily Express	Very strongly UKIP	393
Financial Times	Conservative/Liberal Democrat	189
Guardian	Moderate Labour	157
Independent	Conservative/Liberal democrat	59

Source: YouGov

Knowledge check 14

From the information in Table 43:

- Which party receives most support from newspapers?
- Which are the two most significant newspapers in term of Conservative support?
- Which is the only mass circulation newspaper supporting Labour?

Research suggests that newspapers have relatively little impact on the political views of their readers, but they do, it is believed, reinforce *existing* attitudes. However, there are some concerns about press bias:

- Newspapers may contribute to setting the agenda — identifying certain issues which makes them most significant — and so favour some parties more than others. This often applies to the economy.
- Newspapers may influence people concerning the image of leaders. Ed Miliband suffered a major press campaign in 2015, suggesting he was ineffective.
- The press may influence people's image of the parties in general (valence), which may influence some floating voters.
- Even though newspapers may have little influence over voters, some politicians *believe* they do and so they can be influenced to change their policies to please newspaper proprietors.
- In 2017 Jeremy Corbyn did appear to defy a very negative press image by increasing his standing during the election campaign.

Political opinion polls

The problems concerning **opinion polls** include a number of features. The main issues are as follows:

- The media and political parties pay a great deal of attention to opinion polls.
- In recent elections and referendums, opinion polls have proved to be inaccurate. They failed to predict the Conservative general election victory in 2015, the 'Leave' vote in the 2016 EU referendum and the hung parliament in 2017.
- Voters may adjust their intentions according to what the polls are revealing. For example, some voters may have decided not to vote Labour in 2015 as they feared a Labour–SNP coalition. Some may have voted to leave the EU as a protest as they expected the outcome to be 'Remain' and their vote would not matter.
- If the polls are showing a clear outcome one way or another it may discourage people from voting at all.
- Parties may adjust their policies as a result of opinion poll findings even though they may be inaccurate.

These issues have led to calls for controlling opinion polls. The main proposal is to ban the publication of polls in the run-up to elections. Table 44 summarises the arguments for and against the banning of polls:

Table 44 Should the publication of opinion polls be banned in the run-up to elections?

For banning	Against banning
They may influence the way people vote.	It would infringe the principle of freedom of expression.
They have proved to be inaccurate so they mislead the public.	If they are banned they will become available privately for organisations that can afford to pay for them.
Arguably politicians should not be slaves to changing public opinion as expressed in the polls.	Polls give valuable information about people's attitudes, which can guide politicians usefully.
	They would still be published abroad and people could access them through the internet.

Exam tip

Do not confuse the fact that the press may have influence over politicians, which it probably does, as opposed to voters, which it does to a lesser extent.

Opinion polls Statistical research, carried out by professional organisations, which measures the voting intentions of people as well as their attitudes towards political issues, parties and political leaders.

General election case studies

You should gather material from three general elections, one from 1945–92 (1979 is recommended), the 1997 election and one since 1997 (the most recent election is recommended). In each case you should study the following features of the election:

- What were the main features of the outcome? How did each party perform?
- What were the main changes since the previous election? Which parties gained ground, which lost ground?
- What were the main issues at the election?
- What were the main factors that influenced the outcome? Was it valence issues? Leadership factors? Economic factors? Long-term changes in social factors?
- How was the political system affected by the outcome? Did government change? What was the size of the government majority? Was there a hung parliament?

Summary

When you have completed this topic you should have a thorough knowledge of the following information and issues:

- the influence of social class on voting behaviour
- the concept of partisanship and its decline
- the influence of other social factors on voting behaviour such as age, ethnicity and region
- the importance of rational choice voting, issue voting and economic influences
- the importance of party leadership
- the importance of voter turnout
- the meaning and importance of tactical voting
- the influence of the media on voting
- the role of the media and opinion polls in politics
- the issue of bias in the media
- how to undertake case studies of elections.

In addition, you should have gathered appropriate information to help you answer the following wide-ranging questions:

1 Assess the importance of social class in voting in the UK.
2 Explain the influence of social factors other than class in voting behaviour.
3 To what extent are issues important in the outcome of elections?
4 What is valence and why is it important in elections?
5 Using information about three general elections, what are the most important factors in determining the outcome of elections?
6 Assess the impact of the media in electoral outcomes.
7 Are opinion polls now so unreliable that they should be controlled?

Questions and Answers

How to use this section

This section begins with a guide to the structure of the examination for AS Paper 1 and A-level Paper 1, followed by an explanation of the assessment objectives and guidance on how to use source material and timing your answers. It is important that you familiarise yourself with the exam structure, the nature of assessment objectives and how you can score marks for each of those assessment objectives.

There follow some specimen examination questions. These are neither past examination questions, nor future examination questions, but they are very similar to the kind of questions you will face.

The best way to use this section of the guide is to look at each question and make notes on how you would go about answering it, including the key facts and knowledge you would use, the relevant examples, the analysis, arguments and evaluations you would deploy and the conclusions you would reach. You should also make a plan of how you would answer the whole question, taking account of the tips (indicated by the icon ⓔ) immediately below the question.

After each specimen question there are either one or two exemplar answers. There is a strong answer for all 10-mark questions and both a stronger and weaker answer for the 30-mark A-level answers. The commentary (indicated by the icon ⓔ) that follows it points out each answer's strengths and weaknesses and gives an indication as to how many marks would be awarded for each assessment objective. You should compare these sample answers with your own notes. Amend your notes to bring them to the standard of the stronger sample answers. Having done all this, you can then attempt a full answer to the question, aiming to avoid the weaknesses but including the strengths that have been indicated in the specimen answers and explanation of the marks.

Of course you may use the information in your own way. Remember, however, that simply 'learning' the strong sample answers will not help — these are answers to specimen questions, not the questions you will actually face. It is better to learn *how* to answer questions 'actively', that is by writing your own answers, using the questions and answers included here as a guide. In this way you should then be able to tackle effectively any questions that come your way in the examination.

The structure of the examination

AS Paper 1

Section A: a choice of one from two 10-mark questions.

Section B: two compulsory 10-mark source-based questions. One question focuses on a single source and the other on two comparative sources. The command word for the first of these questions is 'explain' and for the second 'assess'.

Section C: a choice of one from two 30-mark essay questions.

For examples of 30-mark questions, see A-level exemplars. Note, however, that AS and A-level questions have slightly different requirements. AS essay questions always begin with a brief quotation and the words: 'How far do you agree…' while A-level questions always begin with the command word 'Evaluate…'. A-level questions also require relevant knowledge and understanding of UK government and core political ideas.

A-level Paper 1

Section A: one from two source-based 30-mark questions AND one from two 30-mark essay questions.

Section B is a choice of two essay-style questions about non-core political ideas. **This is not covered in this guide** but is covered in Hodder Education's *Edexcel Politics: Political Ideas Student Guide* (978-1-4718-9313-1).

The nature of assessment objectives

Assessment objectives (AOs) refer to the skills you need to demonstrate to gain marks. They involve knowledge and understanding, analysis, evaluation, constructing a coherent answer, using examples and, where appropriate, using material from different parts of the specification. The latter are known as synoptic skills. A detailed explanation of assessment objectives and synoptic skills can be found in the Edexcel specification.

Using source material

With source questions it is important to make reference to the arguments in each source, to evaluate the different arguments presented in the source and to strike a balance between the different views and arguments in the source. When there are two sources for one question, you must make reference to and analyse differences between the two sources.

The distribution of assessment objectives

An explanation of how assessment objective marks are attached to each question plus details of marking levels used by examiners can be found in the Edexcel specification.

Timing your answers

It is obviously important to allocate an appropriate amount of time to answering each question. How much time you should allocate depends on the proportion of the total marks available for each question. Here we assume 5 minutes reading time for each of the source questions. On that basis this guide indicates approximately how much time you should spend answering each question, leaving some spare time to look over your answers at the end.

AS

10-mark questions	15 minutes
30-mark question	45 minutes

A-level

30-mark questions	40 minutes
24-mark questions	33 minutes (*not covered in this guide*)

■ AS-style questions

Democracy and participation

Question 1

Describe direct democracy and illustrate how it operates in the UK.   (10 marks)

ⓔ This question has two parts. Your answer should address both equally. The first part is really asking you to distinguish direct democracy from representative democracy. The second part is clearly largely about referendums so you must demonstrate how they operate. You should include at least one example. Remember that direct democracy operates at several levels in the UK.

Student answer

In contrast to representative democracy, direct democracy is a system where important political and constitutional decisions are made directly by the people rather than by their elected representatives. The best example of direct democracy happened in ancient Athens when important decisions were put to the free citizens who had gathered in the market place. It was also called market place democracy. ⓐ

In modern politics it is not possible for the people to be constantly making decisions so it is left for very important issues to be settled in a referendum. There have been a number of referendums in Britain since they were first used in 1975 to decide whether Britain should remain in the EU. When to hold a referendum is decided by the government though the decision has to be agreed by parliament. Once it has been agreed, the wording of the question is agreed and has to be approved by the Electoral Commission which is in charge of elections and referendums. The question has to be very clear, unbiased and must require a simple yes or no answer. ⓑ Because parliament is sovereign, referendums are not legally binding, the decision must be agreed by parliament, but it is unthinkable that parliament would not agree to a decision made directly by the people.

The next question is ⓒ how they operate in the UK. Referendums are used at local, regional and national levels. Examples of local referendums include whether to introduce congestion charges for motorists in big cities and whether the local council should be allowed to raise council tax above a certain level. The best known regional referendum was the 2014 vote on whether Scotland should be an independent country (rejected) and the devolution votes in 1997 (accepted). National votes are rare but of course the 2016 referendum on EU membership was a huge event with great consequences. There was also a vote on electoral reform in 2011 (rejected). ⓓ

Direct democracy also operates in Switzerland where many issues are settled by referendums and in some states in the USA where they are known as initiatives.

So we can see that the way direct democracy operates in the UK **e** is that only important decisions of a constitutional type are put to a national or regional vote, while local issues that concern taxes may also need the direct approval of the people. However, the fact that the UK uses referendums quite frequently these days does not mean that Britain is a direct democracy. It is still a representative democracy, but it uses direct democratic methods from time to time. **f**

e **10/10 marks awarded.** This is a very full and clear answer. **a** It begins with a comprehensive definition of direct democracy. **b** There is then a useful expansion of the definition and some material on how the system works. A good technique is used **c** when the student refers back to the second part of the question to make it clear where the answer is going. **d** The use of examples is good. Both aspects of the question have been thoroughly dealt with and the explanations are very full. **e** There is a brief conclusion which successfully draws the material together. **f** The final sentence is crucial because it perfectly sums up the position in the UK.

e All marks are for AO1.

Question 2

Read this original material.

Social representation

We tend to think of representation in terms of elections and accountability as well as the representation of interests or constituencies. However, representation can mean something else. This concerns the degree to which representative institutions — parliament, government, parties etc. — reflect the social make-up of the UK. The most obvious example is the fact that women are under-represented in both houses of the UK Parliament and in the government. Members of ethnic minorities also need to be represented. The situation in this regard has improved in recent years but a great deal still needs to be done.

Of course the UK has had, since 2016, a female prime minister for the first time since 1990. This does not guarantee the representation of women in government, but it does indicate a change in attitude towards gender. Finally, we should also consider the age profile of representatives and their social and occupational background. The typical MP is white, middle class and middle aged or elderly.

The House of Lords is even less socially representative. This is not surprising, especially concerning age. Peers are usually at the end of their careers so they are likely to be elderly, but there is no excuse for the lack of women or members of ethnic and religious minorities. The good news is that the Scottish Parliament and Welsh Assembly do have a more representative profile among their memberships.

Using the source, explain how far UK political institutions are socially representative. (10 marks)

In your response you must use knowledge and understanding to analyse points that are only in the source. You will not be rewarded for introducing any additional points that are not in the source.

e The source guides you towards certain important aspects of social representation, i.e. gender and ethnic origin. However, the issues of age and occupational background are also referred to. You should therefore address these four features. The source does not give you any data so you should quote any relevant data you know, e.g. what proportion of MPs are women.

Student answer

The term social representation means that institutions and organisations should reflect society as a whole. This means that such sections of society as women, ethnic minorities, religions and social classes should be fairly represented in such parts of the political system as government, parliament, devolved assemblies and local government. **a**

Perhaps the most important factor is how many women there are in the political system. In theory this should be half. The prime minister is a woman, of course, and she has eight female members of cabinet which is still well short of fair representation. However, when we get to parliament the picture is not so good. About 35% of the House of Commons is made up of women and 25% of the House of Lords. **b** When we look at the Scottish Parliament the position is a little better with 35% women. In local government there are more women which is encouraging. It is also true that most party leaders in the UK today are women which says much for their progress in politics.

Ethnic minorities are not well represented. About 15% of the population are from ethnic minorities, but all political institutions have a lower proportion. In parliament the number is about 8% and there are only two cabinet members. In Scotland only a tiny proportion of members are from ethnic minorities. **c**

It is certainly true that political institutions are filled with mostly middle-class people from the professions. This is totally unrepresentative. **d** There should be a large proportion of working-class members of the various assemblies and in local government. There used to be a time when the Labour Party had many working-class representatives in parliament and in local government, but this is no longer true. This may be a reason why Labour was doing badly — its supporters felt they were not being represented. **e**

When we come to religion there is a further problem. In particular the House of Lords is a case in point. There are 26 bishops of the Church of England but none of the other religions have seats reserved for them. There are some Muslims and Hindus in parliament but they are very under-represented. This is a problem because members of such minorities may feel unrepresented and this causes problems with social unrest, crime and terrorism.

Finally, turning to age, too many representatives are middle aged and elderly. The average age of MPs is 55 and 66 in the House of Lords. This turns people off politics and can account for the low turnout among young people in elections.

Clearly then the British political system is not socially representative. **f**

e **8/10 marks awarded.** This is a solid and comprehensive answer. **a** There is a very good introduction which explains the terms of the question. **b** The student considers a full range of factors and includes a good deal of statistical evidence. **c** It is not always vital to quote exact statistics and this is a case in point where approximate proportions are quoted. **d–f** The section on social class is a little vague which is the answer's only real weakness other than the poor conclusion.

e A01: 4/5 marks, A02: 4/5 marks

For examples of 30-mark questions see A-level exemplars. Note that 30-mark questions for AS will always begin with a brief quotation and the words: 'How far do you agree…'. A-level 30-mark questions always begin with the command 'Evaluate…' However, the content of, and approach to, both kinds of question is essentially similar, although the A-level questions also require relevant knowledge and understanding of UK government and core political ideas.

Political parties

Question 1

Describe the meaning of the term 'left wing' in relation to UK politics. (10 marks)

ⓔ You need to address two issues here. First, what does the term mean 'in general' in terms of ideology and values? This may include socialist ideas. The second aspect requires you to give examples of specific policies which might be considered left wing, such as the nationalisation of major industries (e.g. railways).

Student answer

The term left wing is usually associated with socialism and in particular with the British Labour Party, although Labour has blown hot and cold on left-wing ideas. Under Attlee it was definitely left wing as it was under Foot and Benn, but it moved to the centre under Blair, then moved left again under Corbyn. ⓐ

Probably the most important left-wing idea concerns equality. Marxists, who are the most extreme left wingers, believe in complete equality in living standards, but most socialists in Britain simply believe in reducing inequality by redistributing income. This is mainly done through a progressive tax system and the provision of welfare for those in need. So we have seen a generous benefits system introduced in the last 60 years as well as the provision of free healthcare and education. Left wingers also believe in equality in education. ⓑ

Left wingers see education as vital in creating equality of opportunity. If everyone has an equal chance in life then this is seen as an example of social justice. Social justice is a left-wing idea. It means a fairer society in general. ⓑ

It is a left-wing view that employers have too much power and that workers are generally weak. So a belief in strong workers' rights and strong trade unions is supported. Workers should have the right to take industrial action and should be legally protected from unfair practices and given generous pensions and job security by employers.

When large-scale industries are working against the interests of consumers and workers and the community in general, left wingers often proposed that they be nationalised and brought under state control. This has been done in the past with the railways, coal and steel and a host of other big industries. This means prices can be controlled and employment guaranteed and it stops private companies making excessive profits. ⓒ

Left wingers also share many ideas with liberals such as a democratic society and equal rights for all. This is because they want a fair society where everyone can have an equal influence and is equally protected.

So we can see that the idea of being left wing can mean extreme socialism and Marxism but usually means socialism in general. The Labour Party in the UK has from time to time been left wing in its outlook, but this is not always the case. The Green Party and the SNP are also left-wing parties. d

e **10/10 marks awarded.** This is excellent. It is comprehensive and clear and uses plenty of examples. a There is a brief but useful introduction and then a clear set of examples to show what left wing means. It is a great strength of this answer that it deals in left-wing ideas and not just policies. b There are several sections where the answer explains left-wing ideas and then gives examples of the policies resulting from these ideas. c The description of nationalisation is especially strong. d The conclusion is brief but, like the introduction, gives a useful summary.

e **All marks are for AO1.**

Question 2 (two-source question)

Read this original material.

Source 1

Party factions

It is often argued that the conflicts within parties are more significant than conflicts between parties. This is particularly true of the Conservative Party over recent years. The main problem has concerned Europe. The eurosceptics in the party have constantly caused problems for the leadership and, even after the referendum signalled the UK's exit from the EU, they continued to demand a 'hard Brexit'.

Of course, since 2015, Labour has suffered similar problems. Many new 'left wingers' joined the party in 2015–16 and they elected Jeremy Corbyn to the leadership with a mandate to pursue radical socialist policies. The problem is that most Labour MPs and peers do not share this vision of the party's policies. One leadership challenge failed in 2016 and this schism between left wingers and moderates looks set to dog the party for some time to come.

Source 2

Parties as broad coalitions

The idea that a political party in the UK is a single entity with a single political philosophy is actually an illusion. All parties are coalitions of different groups. These groups may share an overarching philosophy but stress different aspects of their political tradition.

Thus the Labour Party contains members who are pure socialists and others who are moderate 'Blairite' social democrats. There are also members whose main concern is trade unionism. The Conservatives contain traditionalists, sometimes known as one-nation Tories, as well as

Thatcherites who combine neo-liberalism with neo-conservatism. Under Cameron the party became even more varied with modern liberal progressive conservatives coming to the fore. Even the Liberal Democrats have different wings. The party was formed from an amalgamation of the Social Democratic Party and the former Liberal Party.

This feature of modern parties can be seen as a virtue. It means they can attract a wider range of support and gives them a richer and more sensitive aspect which can be attractive to voters.

Questions and Answers

Using the sources, assess the extent to which factionalism within parties can adversely affect their fortunes.

(10 marks)

In your response you must compare both sources by analysing and evaluating them and any knowledge must support this analysis and evaluation in order to gain credit.

ⓔ You need to define factionalism — the sources will help you to do that. The sources also provide you with two major examples. You do not need to quote other examples. However, you do need to explain how these factional problems have affected the fortunes of Labour and the Conservatives. Your answer must address the fact that the two sources have very different perspectives on factionalism and you should attempt some assessment of the relative value of the two views.

A party faction is a group within a party who disagree fundamentally with the main policies of the party. Sometimes a faction will even have a formal organisation like 'Momentum' which represents left wingers in Labour. There are also formal factions in the Conservative Party and some factionalism in the Liberal Democrats. The question is — do such factions damage parties or are they just a normal part of politics? ⓐ

Source 2 sees such factions as a positive feature in a number of ways and it is true that such variations are inevitable in political parties. It is also true that a wide-ranging party will attract support from different quarters so the Labour Party wins votes from trade unionists, from workers in general and from middle-class people in caring professions. The Conservative Party also wins support from both the working classes and middle classes because it is a 'broad church'. However, we must also remember that voting behaviour theory suggests that voters tend not to support parties which appear to be divided. ⓑ This means the positive effect of being a broad party is cancelled out by the effect of being a divided party. Probably the answer lies in how deep the divisions are and whether the party can produce a single, unified policy at elections. This is something Labour has certainly struggled to do. ⓒ

The main problem for divided parties is that, if they get into power, they cannot rely on the support of their own members which means that government is weak. This happened to John Major in the 1990s when some of his party (he called them the 'bastards') were opposed to his policy of closer integration with the European Union through the Maastricht Treaty. In fact he once resigned so that he could be re-elected to maintain his authority. In the end this may have led to his defeat in the election in 1997. It also used to happen to Labour governments when the leadership was hindered by left-wing factions. ⓓ

The second problem is that voters do not like divided parties. This is called valence in voting behaviour theory. The image of a party is very important and a divided party has a divided and weak image. ⓑ The Conservative Party was still factionalised after it lost power in 1997 and the party lost three elections in a row. When the Corbyn faction took over Labour after 2015 the party's fortunes collapsed and they were well behind in the opinion polls (though it recovered by 2017). The main Labour faction is Momentum which is a left-wing group.

A third problem with factions is that parties find it difficult to form agreed policies if they are divided by factions. The main example has been the Conservative Party under Theresa May finding it difficult to agree a policy on exiting the EU and making a new agreement with them. Fortunately for them, the Labour Party is even more divided by factions and so the opposition is very weak.

Even the Liberal Democrats have factions. The Orange Book group favour policies of free markets and this is not in agreement with the social democrats in the party. This is also holding them back. In contrast the SNP is very united and this shows in its electoral victories and general popularity in Scotland.

Thus we can see that factionalism is a serious problem for parties for three main reasons. It makes it difficult for them to govern, it makes it difficult for them to be elected and it is harder to develop agreed policies. United parties without major factions have a big advantage. **e**

e **10/10 marks awarded.** The main strength of this excellent answer is that it addresses the question, which is not asking you to describe factions, but to explain the impact that factionalism has on parties. **a** The introduction clearly shows this by defining factionalism and then stating that the answer will address the problems that arise. It is good practice to introduce material from another part of the course (known as synopticity). This is done at two points marked **b** where voting behaviour is introduced. **c** The student addresses the different issues in both sources and makes a certain amount of comparison and assessment between the two. There is then a clear progression though three distinct issues. **d** This section clearly describes a problem in relation to a specific example. **e** Having successfully explained three impacts the answer concludes with a summary paragraph.

e **AO1: 5/5 marks, AO2: 5/5 marks**

For examples of 30-mark questions see A-level exemplars. Note that 30-mark questions for AS will always begin with a brief quotation and the words: 'How far do you agree…'. A-level 30-mark questions always begin with the command 'Evaluate…' However, the content of, and approach to, both kinds of question is essentially similar, although the A-level questions also require relevant knowledge and understanding of UK government and core political ideas.

Electoral systems

Question 1

Describe the main features of the first-past-the-post electoral system. (10 marks)

e You need to explain how the system works and also what the various impacts of the system are. The impacts include the way it affects party representation as well as the general outcome of elections in terms of government formation. Some data from recent elections will be very useful.

Student answer

First past the post (FPTP) is the name commonly given to the plurality system which is used in UK general elections. This answer will explain how the system actually works and then will explain why it has the effects that it does. **a**

FPTP is a plurality system which means that the candidate who received most votes wins the election. A candidate does not need to win an overall majority and in fact only about half the MPs in parliament won over 50% of the votes in their seat. It is a simple system because voters find it easy to understand that they have just one vote and they can choose the candidate from the party they support. It is also very easy to count and the results are known rapidly. **b**

The more important factor in FPTP is the kind of results that it produces. First it prevents most small party candidates from winning seats. This is because there is only one winner in each seat. Parties that come second or third in many seats, like the Liberal Democrats, win very few seats. This means that the system favours parties whose supporters are concentrated in some areas and works against parties with dispersed support. Therefore the Conservatives, Labour and the SNP in Scotland are advantaged by the system but UKIP and the Green Party suffer a great deal.

It also leads to many wasted votes because in safe seats the result is a foregone conclusion. In marginal seats, where the result is in doubt, voters have a strong influence and their vote is not wasted. On the plus side the system means that the House of Commons is dominated by two parties and it is nearly always the case that one of the parties wins an overall majority and can form a stable government. This did not work in 2010 when there was a hung parliament, but this used to be a rare event.

Another feature of the system is that voters find it easy and it is popular, evidenced by the rejection of AV in the 2011 referendum.

Finally, an important feature is that it makes a very strong link between the MP and the constituents. In some systems there are no constituencies or more than one representative for each seat so this confuses voters, but we all know who our MP is. **c**

In conclusion, the main features of FPTP are that it is an easy to understand system with clear results and a strong constituency system. On the other hand, it is also unfair to small parties and makes votes have unequal value. **d**

e **9/10 marks awarded.** This is not perfectly written but it is good enough to earn nearly full marks. **a** The introduction sets out the two key parts of the answer. The student addresses the features and not just the workings of the system. **b** The description of the workings is clear enough. There are then a series of features which are well described. **c** By the time we come to the conclusion we have a clear view of what the features are. **d** Finally, there is a conclusion which summarises the system, both its good and its criticised features.

e **All marks are for AO1.**

Question 2 (two-source question)

Read this original material.

Source 1

2015 general election: average votes needed to elect one member   *Does not include the Speaker's seat

Party	Total votes won nationally (a)	Seats won nationally (b)	Average votes per winning candidate (a) ÷ (b)
UKIP	3,881,099	1	3,881,099
Green Party	1,157,630	1	1.157,613
Liberal Democrats	2,415,916	8	301,989
Plaid Cymru	181,704	3	60,568
Ulster Unionists	114,935	2	57,468
Sinn Fein	176,232	4	44,058
Labour	9,347,273	232	40,290
Conservative	11,334,226	331	34,243
SDLP (NI)	99,810	3	33,270
SNP	1,454,436	56	25,972
Democratic Unionists	184,260	8	23,033
Total	30,347,521	649*	46,760

Source 2

Many critics of the first-past-the-post system claim that it leads to votes being of unequal value. However, there is another perspective on this issue. This is that votes are actually of the same value. There is one person one vote and every voter understands exactly how the system works. The fact that some seats are safe and others are marginal is actually irrelevant. If a candidate gains more votes than any of his or her rivals it is obviously fair that the candidate should be elected. Voters are also free to vote tactically and so increase the value of their vote. Each constituency is also a separate contest so all votes count the same *within* the constituency.

Using the sources, assess the extent to which votes were of unequal value in the 2015 UK general election.

(10 marks)

In your response you must compare both sources by analysing and evaluating them and any knowledge must support this analysis and evaluation in order to gain credit.

ⓔ You need to look at the data and explain what they are actually showing. Having explained what unequal value means, you need to explain why first past the post tends to result in such outcomes in terms of safe seats and discrimination against smaller parties. It is good technique to pick out a few key statistics from the sources to illustrate your answer.

Student answer

It is clear from Source 1 that votes were very much of unequal value at the 2015 general election. The fact that UKIP won only one seat despite gaining 3.8 million votes makes a UKIP vote almost worthless. By contrast a vote for the SNP in Scotland was incredibly valuable because it took on average only 25,000 votes to elect each MP. Similarly votes for the Green Party and the Liberal Democrats were worth far less than votes for the two main parties. **ⓐ**

There are several reasons why votes were of unequal value as shown in the data given. The first is the fact that under FPTP there are rewards for parties which have very concentrated support (e.g. SNP, Conservatives, Labour) in terms of seats won, but a huge disadvantage to parties whose support is spread widely (e.g. Greens, Lib Dems). **b** This is because the parties with concentrated support come first in many constituencies whereas those with dispersed support often come second or third which wins them no seats. This means that votes for such parties as the Conservatives, Labour and SNP are worth more than votes for the Greens and Lib Dems. **c**

Another reason for unequal value is the fact that there are many safe seats. A safe seat is one where only one party can realistically win and that party wins at every election. Henley is an example of a safe Conservative seat while Jeremy Corbyn's seat in London is a safe Labour seat. Marginal seats are those where the result is likely to be close. Therefore voters in marginal seats have a better chance of affecting the outcome. Their votes are more valuable than those of voters in safe seats who cannot affect the result.

It is also generally true that votes for small parties are less valuable than those for large parties, not just because of the data, but because small parties have no hope of forming a government so their policies will never be implemented. The only time this was not the case was when the Lib Dems were brought into a coalition government in 2010.

Source 2 makes a case for suggesting that votes in individual constituencies are equal in value, but this does not take into account the fact that a general election is a national contest, not just a series of constituency elections. It could be argued that it is unfortunate if a voter supports a small party with no chance of winning, but that is the free choice of the voter. If a voter wishes to increase the value of his or her vote they can simply change to one of the main parties and they may also choose to vote tactically to make their vote more effective. **d**

So, despite Source 2, the main reason votes are of unequal value is that it takes so many more votes to elect on average candidates from some parties such as UKIP, but many fewer votes to elect a Conservative, Labour or SNP member. However, in addition there are issues concerning too many safe seats and the disadvantages suffered by small parties. **e**

e **10/10 marks awarded.** This is an excellent answer worthy of full marks. **a** At the beginning it directly addresses both the question and the data, explaining what the data are showing. **b** It then continues by addressing the question further with two more substantial arguments which are explained fully and clearly. **c** It continually returns to the subject of the question. **d** The answer also engages with both sources and examines the differences between them critically. It is acceptable to reject one of the contentions, as is done in this answer, as long as this approach is justified. **e** Finally, there is a very good conclusion, which again directly addresses the question.

e **AO1: 5/5 marks, AO2: 5/5 marks**

For examples of 30-mark questions see A-level exemplars. Note that 30-mark questions for AS will always begin with a brief quotation and the words: 'How far do you agree…'. A-level 30-mark questions always begin with the command 'Evaluate…' However, the content of, and approach to, both kinds of question is essentially similar, although the A-level questions also require relevant knowledge and understanding of UK government and core political ideas.

Voting behaviour and the media

Question 1

Describe the meaning of the terms partisan dealignment and class dealignment.   (10 marks)

ⓔ A straightforward two-part answer is needed here and you should give equal attention to each half. You need to explain what the terms mean and then explain why they are important in explaining voting behaviour. (This is an unusual question as it is in two parts. Both parts are worth at least 4 marks, but the question is worth more than 8 marks in total.)

> **Student answer**
>
> Partisan dealignment is something that has been growing over the past few decades. When research into voting behaviour began in the 1960s it was very predictable how people would vote as it depended almost totally on their social class. It was also true that nearly everyone was either working class or middle class and there were only two significant parties — Labour and Conservative. So it was inevitable that the middle classes voted Conservative and the working class voted for Labour. ⓐ This meant that people had a very close association with the party that represented their class. In fact many people were members of that party and members of the working class were often in a trade union which gave them an even closer association with Labour. It was also true that most people voted the way their parents voted, so attachment to a party was passed down from one generation to the next. ⓑ
>
> Since then there has been a steady change. Fewer and fewer people associate closely with a party. This is partly because of disillusionment with their performance and partly because people are more likely to change their allegiance. We are now in the age of the floating voter and the instrumental voter. Instrumental voting is where voters look at the policies of the parties and decide which is best for themselves or for the community as a whole. This is also called the rational model of voting. It is also true that the class system has broken down so class and party allegiance are now weaker, even though about 40% vote for the party that represents their class. This brings us on to the other fact causing this which is class dealignment. ⓒ
>
> Class dealignment is where people do not associate closely with one class. In other words, they see themselves as an individual and not a member of a class. In particular many fewer people consider themselves to be working class. The middle class has also fragmented into different sections. There are also many who are a member of one class according to their occupation but who do not

Questions and Answers

think of themselves in that way. Class dealignment means that people do not behave as we would expect. In particular it no longer helps us to predict so well how they will vote. Many members of the working class today vote Conservative or UKIP and middle-class people vote Liberal Democrat or Green. d

So we can see that class dealignment and partisan dealignment are closely linked and the first has an impact on the second. e

e **9/10 marks awarded**. There is only one weakness in this excellent answer — its conclusion. It was a good idea to link the two concepts in this way but it should be developed further, perhaps by discussing class and voting a little more. a, b The answer begins well by explaining the links between class and voting. c It is a good technique to link one point with the next as is done here. This is not always possible or appropriate but should be done if the opportunity arises. d, e Class dealignment is described well and then the limited conclusion drops just 1 mark.

e All marks are for AO1.

Question 2

Read this original material.

The media and politics in the UK

It is often said that the UK enjoys a 'free press'. This means that there is no influence exerted by the government or politicians in general on the newspapers. However, it does not mean that the newspapers are neutral; far from it. Virtually all newspapers in the UK demonstrate a clear political bias. In most cases their proprietors and editors argue that they are merely reflecting the typical political attitudes of their typical readers.

Some papers, such as the *Daily Telegraph*, *Daily Mail* and *Daily Mirror*, always support the same party, whereas others, such as the *Sun*, *Independent* and *The Times*, can vary in their attitudes to parties. Certainly all papers show a preference on the eve of elections and urge their readers to vote this way or that. The big question is: does this have any significant impact on voters? The *Sun* claimed to have won the 1992 election for the Conservatives

against all odds, but then supported Labour before its landslide victory in 1997.

Ahead of the referendum on EU membership in 2016 the newspapers recommended to their readers how they should vote. The papers with large circulations, notably the *Sun* and *Daily Mail*, both urged a 'Leave' vote. The real question remains, however, whether the newspapers were leading public opinion or were following it.

The growing importance of social media may also be reflected in political views. Of course the internet and social media are free and open so any political views can be disseminated. This makes its influence difficult to assess.

Turning to broadcast media it must be stressed that all broadcasters have a statutory requirement to be neutral so it seems unlikely that they have any significant influence which might affect the fortunes of parties or the outcome of a referendum.

Using the source, explain how much the media influence political attitudes in the UK. (10 marks)

In your response you must use knowledge and understanding to analyse points that are only in the source. You will not be rewarded for introducing any additional points that are not in the source.

62 **Edexcel Politics**

(e) The source gives you useful information about the political bias of newspapers, but does not actually explain the degree to which they have influence over voting behaviour. You need to use your own knowledge to assess what influence the press may have. You can speculate rather than coming to firm conclusions as this is a contentious issue.

Student answer

The influence of the press in Britain has long been a controversial issue. As the source mentions it is not clear whether the press influences people's political attitudes and voting in particular or whether newspapers are simply reflecting the views of their readers to encourage them to buy the paper. This needs to be examined as does the impact of social media. The source says that the broadcast media are neutral by law in Britain and there is no evidence that they have any influence one way or another, even though some say the BBC has a left-wing bias. It is not worth examining the broadcasters therefore and we should concentrate on print and social media. a

At elections and referendums the newspapers do normally recommend their readers to vote one way or another. There is no conclusive evidence whether this influences their readers. Evidence suggests it does not because, if it did, the Conservatives would always win every election because most of the big circulation newspapers support the Tories. b The papers that support Labour are shrinking and so Labour should have no chance in the future. Fortunately for Labour the *Sun* sometimes supports it as it did in 1997. There certainly was a huge press campaign against Jeremy Corbyn, which was damaging to him in 2015–17 (though he recovered his reputation during the 2017 campaign).

It cannot be concluded that the press does or does not significantly affect political attitudes and even the editors and owners like Paul Dacre (*Mail*) and Murdoch (*Sun*, *The Times*) say that they are not trying to influence but simply reflect the attitude of readers. c Not surprisingly, the Labour Party does complain that the 'Tory press' is a conspiracy against it, but that is to be expected. d

Turning to social media the position is very mixed. As the source says social media is free to all and we all have access. e This means that all sorts of political views are being peddled. It is likely that political attitudes are being formed, especially with big e-petition campaigns such as over Brexit and anti-fracking etc. but this is about single issues. There is probably no significant bias in social media concerning political parties. However, the big wave of support for Corbyn in 2015 was probably fostered by a big social media campaign against Miliband and pro-Corbyn. Half a million people joined the Labour Party as a result. f

So we can see that this is a very difficult issue to resolve. This is because the research does not reveal a great deal and the evidence we have points in two directions. It is logical that the newspapers must have some influence, but the real question is how much? g

e **10/10 marks awarded.** This is a very good response to a difficult question. **a** It starts with a good summary of how the student is going to answer the question and refers to the source. **b** Evidence is important even though it does not have to be precise. Any cogent evidence, as is used here, is useful. **c**, **d** These sentences provide two excellent pieces of broad evidence. **e** On social media the answer refers again to the source without actually quoting from it (which you should not do). **f** This is an excellent and topical point. **g** The conclusion expresses the problem of conflicting evidence and summarises the analysis successfully.

e **AO1: 5/5 marks, AO2: 5/5 marks**

For examples of 30-mark questions see A-level exemplars. Note that 30-mark questions for AS will always begin with a brief quotation and the words: 'How far do you agree…'. A-level 30-mark questions always begin with the command 'Evaluate…' However, the content of, and approach to, both kinds of question is essentially similar, although the A-level questions also require relevant knowledge and understanding of UK government and core political ideas.

■ A-level-style questions

Democracy and participation

Question 1

Read this original material.

> **Turnout at elections**
>
> Low turnouts in UK elections and referendums have become a serious cause for concern. Many argue that democracy will decline if people do not participate in large numbers. One proposed solution is to introduce compulsory voting. This has been done in Australia and turnouts there are now above 90%. Compulsory voting reflects the idea that voting is a civic duty so we can justify forcing people to vote. It is also probably true that larger turnouts will produce a more representative electorate. As things stand in the UK it is the elderly who vote in large numbers, while the young tend to stay at home. This distorts the outcome of elections and referendums.
>
> Falling turnout has accompanied a significant reduction in party membership and increasing disillusionment with party politics. However, it can also be said that low turnouts are not as important as we think. Those who do not vote, it
>
> could be said, have voluntarily opted out of the democratic process. It may also be said that non-voters are likely to be ignorant about political issues. It is also true that wider political activity is actually on the increase. What is happening is that increasingly large numbers of people see pressure group activity and participation in social media campaigns as more meaningful forms of activity. In fact, it is on the internet and in social media that activity is increasing to the greatest extent.
>
> Nevertheless, turnout remains an important issue. In particular, low turnouts call into question the democratic legitimacy of those who are elected. There is also the changing issue of how *intensive* participation is. Taking part in social media and internet campaigns may count as activity but it is shallow and does not indicate any great engagement with politics.

Using the source, evaluate the view that the UK is suffering from a 'participation crisis'.

(30 marks)

In your response you must:

- ■ *compare the different opinions in the source*
- ■ *consider this view and the alternative to this view in a balanced way*
- ■ *use knowledge and understanding to help you analyse and evaluate*

ⓔ In your introduction you need to explain the term 'participation crisis'. Ideally you should follow this with some information about how participation is indeed falling. Your answer should fall into two parts, both of which are evaluations. First, how much is participation falling and are some types of falling participation being compensated for by rising participation in other ways? Second, you need to address the issue of whether it is a 'crisis'. How important is participation? Has it reached crisis levels? In your answer it is especially important that you refer to material and evidence from other parts of the course, notably the sections on political parties and electoral systems.

Questions and Answers

Student A

Participation can take a number of forms. The most important example is voting in elections and at referendums. However this is not the only example of participation. Many people are also members of political parties and are active supporters, campaigning in elections and generally campaigning for the party. Third, participation can involve pressure groups and campaigning on various issues. This is perhaps the most active form of participation. The question here is whether there is a problem for our democracy over a lack of participation. **a**

The source refers to falling turnout and this has become quite serious. In past decades turnout at general elections used to stand at about 75% but this has fallen to about 60% in recent elections. The main reason this is a problem is that it may reduce the legitimacy of the elected government. In the 2015 election, for example, the Conservative government was elected by just about 23% of the adult population. This was partly because it won only 37% of the vote and partly because the turnout was less than two thirds. However, the turnout at recent referendums has been quite good with well over 70% voting in the EU campaign and referendum on Scottish independence. Then again the referendum on electoral reform in 2011 only attracted about 40% of the adult vote. **b** Even the slight increase in turnout in the 2017 general election has not altered the general picture.

Membership of parties has also been falling. Back in the 1980s there were over 2 million members of political parties whereas now the figure is closer to 0.5 million. There has been an increase in membership of some parties like the Greens and Lib Dems but Conservative membership has fallen. There are many new Labour Party members but it is suspected that most people who joined did so only to elect Jeremy Corbyn. They are really supporters rather than members and it cost very little to register. However, it is a form of participation it has to be said. There is a great deal of disillusionment with political parties and this shows in their falling membership and activity.

On the other hand, there is a great deal of interest in pressure groups. Some pressure groups like Greenpeace and the RSPB have millions of members. These pressure groups are concerned with particular issues, not policies in general which are supported by parties. Members and supporters of pressure groups are active in a number of ways including taking part in demonstrations, lobbying parliament and organising civil disobedience in some cases.

Perhaps the problem is mainly that participation is falling more among the young than the older generation. The 65+ age group still votes in large numbers but voting among the young is especially low. However, on the other hand, the young are much more likely to be active in a pressure group. Campaigns such as anti-fracking, anti-airport expansion and anti-capitalism have been extremely intensive and mostly conducted by the young. **c**

The source describes a number of ways in which participation might be increased but it seems unlikely that these will improve the situation. After all, if voting is compulsory it does not mean that people are engaged with politics, merely that they want to avoid a fine.

In summary then we can say that political participation is certainly declining. There are signs that it is picking up in terms of pressure group activity but overall the fall in voting numbers and the decline in party membership outweigh this. **d**

e 15/30 marks awarded. This is a disappointing answer as **b** the student clearly knows how to construct a logical evaluation and **c** is in possession of a number of key pieces of evidence. **a** The introduction defines participation well enough, but then does not address the question. The weaknesses of the answer then develop. There is a solid enough evaluation with evidence on both sides of the issue, but it lacks two features. The first is that it does not discuss activity in social media and the internet. This is referred to in the source so there is no excuse. The second is that it does not really address the question of whether this amounts to a crisis. In other words, there is no evaluation of how severe the problem may be. **d** There is a conclusion, but it is very limited and does not address the 'crisis' issue.

e A01: 5/10 marks, A02: 5/10 marks, A03: 5/10 marks

Student B

In 2005 turnout at the general election fell to below 60% and this was on top of low turnouts at local and devolved elections. The incident led to a general sense that there was a crisis in political participation. Participation is more than just voting. It is also about being a member and being active in a political party. This too has been falling. Fortunately, just as traditional forms of participation have been falling, new ways in which people can become involved in parties have begun to emerge. So there are two questions to be addressed here. The first is to undertake an evaluation into political participation and the second is to determine how serious the fall off in traditional participation actually is. **a**

Turnout at elections has been low, falling to a typical 60%, although this rose to 65% in 2015 and slightly more in 2017, and there were big turnouts for the referendums in Scotland and over EU membership. This appears to be very serious unless we examine it more closely. Turnout among older voters remains very high and nearly 80% of the older age group turn out to vote typically. The real problem, though, is low turnout among the young. In the 18–24 age group turnout has dropped to below 40%. This is indeed a crisis because it suggests that the situation will grow worse in the future. Even when the young voted in larger numbers in 2017 (nearly 60%), this age group still lags behind the others. **b** As the source says, low turnouts distort the outcome of elections. The Conservatives in 2015 were returned to power by only 23% of the adult population. If we think about young voters, the government has minimal active support. The Labour Party is even claiming that it has captured the imagination of the young under Jeremy Corbyn because its membership shot up when it reduced the membership fee and there was a real issue to engage them — whether to elect a new left-wing leader. The claim here is that the low turnout among the young and higher turnout among the elderly make the UK appear to be a more Conservative country than it really is. **c** This was also demonstrated in the EU referendum when the Leave vote was largely the result of such differential turnout.

Party membership has been falling but this tide may have turned. Membership of smaller parties such as the Greens, UKIP and the SNP did increase after 2010. In fact UKIP has attracted many people who have never voted before. There is also the rise in Labour membership and it claims to be the biggest political party in Europe. However, there is a question of how intensively these new party members are actually involved. Recently, too, membership of Labour has begun to decline again. Perhaps many only joined to elect Corbyn and are not really interested in politics.

We know of course that membership of pressure groups has grown to counter-balance these trends. This may be due to the fact that many people, especially the young, see politics in terms of single issues rather than in terms of party policies. Issues such as the environment, the conduct of capitalism and welfare issues are attracting a great deal of new activity. Large numbers of people have been attracted to demonstrations, acts of civil disobedience, e-petitions and internet campaigns. In fact the internet has opened up a whole new range of opportunities to participate in one kind of political campaign or another. **d**

We do need to think also about referendums. These have become more common and give people an extra opportunity to be involved in politics. How many take advantage of it is mixed. Turnout at the EU referendum and over Scottish independence was high at well above 70%, but other referendums have attracted turnouts as low as 40%.

However, voting in referendums and signing e-petitions or adding one's name to a petition are not really very active forms of participation. Party membership — the most serious form of decline — is a much more intensive kind of activity so it is the most significant of the factors involved. Low levels of participation on social media are of much less importance. Meanwhile the fall in voting numbers, especially among the young, challenges democratic legitimacy. Perhaps, therefore, it is voting figures that should concern us most. In this regard it may well be the unfairness of the electoral system that is causing the problem. **e**

In conclusion there is a crisis in participation which largely involves voting turnout among the young. However, this is reduced by the fact that alternative forms of participation are growing, especially on social media.

e 26/30 marks awarded. This is a strong response which misses out on full marks for a few small reasons. Its main weakness is that it does not fully address the question of whether there is a crisis. This is reflected in its AO3 marks. The student also does not use quite enough examples to underpin the evaluation, so 2 marks are dropped for AO1. Fortunately the analysis is very good, so it scores full marks for AO2.

a The introduction is clear and shows how the question is to be answered. **b** There is some excellent evaluation and **c** the answer makes use of the source. A good illustration of where insufficient examples are used is provided at **d** when discussing pressure groups. The analysis is up to date and shows knowledge of recent developments. **e** The conclusion really spreads over the last two paragraphs but the final brief paragraph is slightly weak. It would be better if the final two paragraphs were amalgamated into one as it would look more precise and thorough.

e AO1: 8/10 marks, AO2: 10/10 marks, AO3: 8/10 marks

Question 2

Evaluate the view that the UK political system is no longer truly representative.   (30 marks)

You must consider this view and the alternative to this view in a balanced way.

(e) There is more than one way in which representation can be defined. You should address this in your introduction. Three main considerations need to be examined here. First, the extent to which different political views are represented in the system (i.e. how well are different parties represented). This will also require material from the section of the course that deals with electoral systems. Second, how well are sectional interests, especially minorities, represented? Third, how socially representative are UK political institutions such as parties, government and parliament? Note that the question says 'no longer'. This implies that things may have been different in the past. This should be reflected in your answer.

Student A

There are different views about how representative the UK system is and this essay will examine both sides of the argument. (a)

The main issue about representation in the UK concerns the electoral system. The first-past-the-post system works in a way which means that the outcome of elections is not truly representative. There are a number of aspects to be described here. First, the system means that the Conservatives, Labour and the SNP are hugely over-represented. The Conservatives won about 37% of the votes but were rewarded with just over 50% of the seats. The SNP won 50% of the Scottish vote but won nearly all the seats. On the other hand, UKIP won nearly 4 million votes and only one seat so it is hopelessly under-represented. The Green Party and the Liberal Democrats also suffered at the hands of the electoral system so they are very much under-represented. (b)

We should also note that the Conservative government does not really represent the majority. It was elected by only 23% of the adult population because two thirds of the electorate did not vote at all. Labour won an even smaller proportion of adult support but is considered to be the official opposition.

Fortunately representation is better in the devolved assemblies. This is because they use forms of proportional representation. This means that in Scotland, for example, all the parties have seats which are broadly representative of party support. The SNP, for example, won just under half of the votes and also just under half of the seats. Labour and the Conservatives also have their fair share. The same applies to Wales and Northern Ireland where STV is used.

Turning to the House of Lords the system is very unrepresentative. The Lords are of course, not even elected so how can they claim to be representative? Furthermore, 92 of them are hereditary peers who owe their position to an accident of birth. Most of these are elderly men from middle-class backgrounds so they are not at all representative of the whole population. (c)

So we can see that the UK system is not very representative at all. This is mainly due to the electoral system for general elections and the totally unrepresentative nature of the House of Lords. (d)

Questions and Answers

ⓔ **12/30 marks awarded.** This is a weak answer for several reasons. One noticeable trait is that it is out of date and does not use data from the 2017 general election. In addition, it only deals with two aspects of representation. It ignores two important aspects of the question — the representation of sectional interests and the degree to which institutions are socially representative. ⓑ It does deal with the effects of first past the post well enough and ⓒ introduces the House of Lords quite effectively, but overall this is a very limited response. ⓐ The introduction is weak and ⓓ the conclusion is even weaker. They scarcely address the question at all.

ⓔ **A01: 4/10 marks, A02: 4/10 marks, A03: 4/10 marks**

Student B

The term representation has a number of meanings. The first concerns the appropriate representation of parties in various institutions. The second concerns the extent to which political institutions are socially represented. In other words, how well do they mirror the demographic distribution of the whole population? Third, there is the extent to which various sections of society are properly represented and protected. This essay will examine these questions and in doing so will try to demonstrate whether the situation is improving or growing worse. ⓐ

If we look at representation in the UK parliament there are serious problems. These have grown worse since the decline of the strict two-party system ⓑ when there were two main parties which divided the seats in accordance with the voting. Now there are several smaller parties which won substantial votes but which have not won their fair share of the seats. UKIP especially suffered in 2015 when the party won 3.8 million votes but won only one seat. In contrast, the Conservatives won just over half of the seats with just 38% of the national vote. The SNP is a smaller party in national terms (not in Scottish terms) but is hugely over-represented in that it won nearly all the Scottish seats on 50% of the vote in that country. It has to be said, of course, that such anomalies were reduced in 2017. Indeed the Labour Party won almost exactly the same proportion of seats as votes. Nevertheless, it is still true that the parties with concentrated support are over-represented and the parties with dispersed support are under-represented. Fortunately, the devolved assemblies are significantly more representative in this regard. ⓑ

Turning to demographics we can certainly say the situation has improved ⓒ. There was a time when there were virtually no women in important positions. Now Britain has its second woman prime minister and about 25% of both the House of Commons and House of Lords are women. There is also good representation of women in local and devolved government. The cabinet also has more women these days compared to a sprinkling before 1997. The vast majority of party leaders throughout Britain are now women and that is huge progress towards representation. Theresa May originally appointed eight women to her cabinet. However, this is still not properly representative and even the Labour Party does not have enough women in its higher positions.

The position on ethnic minorities is similar to women. They are under-represented, but the situation is improving. In the Commons and the Lords the proportion of members of ethnic minorities is about half of what it is in the whole population. A few government ministers are from ethnic minorities and the London mayor is now a British Asian Muslim.

Turning to age and class the institutions are also not representative. Indeed the proportion of people from working-class origins in government and parliament is declining so things are getting worse. It is inevitable that our representatives will be older than the average as we need people with experience. However, the position in the House of Lords, with an average age of 66, is especially serious. Young people are not as committed to politics as they used to be (see voting figures) so we should expect them to be under-represented in parliament. In Scotland and Wales, however, many more young people are being elected. The SNP has many young members like Mhairi Black who was only 20 when first elected.

When we come to sectional interests it could be argued that they are better represented than ever before. The House of Lords contains many of their representatives. All major occupations and pressure groups are represented there. The House of Lords is also becoming more effective in defending interests when scrutinising legislation. The same is not true of the Commons where the party whips still rule, but fortunately growing pressure group and social media activity means that such interest groups receive a good deal of extra parliamentary representation. In fact this is possibly the greatest area of progress. **c**

We can summarise by suggesting that very gradually Britain is becoming more representative than it used to be in two ways — in terms of demographics and sectional interests, but is deteriorating in others — in terms of party representation in parliament. However, there is a great distance to go, especially when we think about the representation of women and ethnic minorities, not to mention minority religions. Representation is a strong feature of British democracy, but it is not really strong enough. **d**

e **30/30 marks awarded.** This is a very strong response worthy of full marks. **a** There is an excellent introduction followed by a full analysis which employs plenty of evidence and material from various sections of the whole course. **b** The section on party representation is also very well covered. **c** A special strength is the way the answer shows how change is taking place, mostly improvements but also that there is still some progress to be made in various regards. **d** Finally, there is a very strong and cogent conclusion which reflects the whole evaluation and comes to a firm summary.

e **A01: 10/10 marks, A02: 10/10 marks, A03: 10/10 marks**

Political parties

Question 1

Read this original material.

The Corbyn revolution

There are two ways of viewing the 'Corbyn revolution' which emerged within the Labour Party in 2015–16. Some argue that this a return to the roots of the Labour Party. Many of Corbyn's ideas were forged in the 1970s and 1980s when he was a young party member and when such ideological figures as Tony Benn, Ken Livingstone and Michael Foot were prominent in the party. His proposals for the state ownership of the railways and state control over utility industries come straight from that era. He also believes in the power of the state to create greater economic equality and to curb the excesses of capitalism.

Others see it as a temporary insurgency. They view the many new supporters who voted for Corbyn in the leadership elections as Marxist 'entryists'. For such critics, the legacy of Tony Blair and New Labour is where the modern Labour Party is and should position itself. They point out that most Labour voters are actually moderate and that the majority of Labour MPs and peers do not support Corbyn. They support more centrist policies on taxation, welfare and the role of the state. This suggests that New Labour and the 'Third Way' are how we should view Labour's roots. This is a very great contrast with the kind of 'British socialism' espoused by the likes of Clement Attlee, Harold Wilson or Tony Benn.

Then, of course, came the 2017 general election at which Labour, under the much-criticised Corbyn, increased its share of the vote by nearly 10%. This gave great encouragement to the left, but the divide in the party still remains. Labour did not win the 2017 election and so is likely to be out of power for up to 12 years.

It remains to be seen whether Labour can survive this split and, indeed, which ideological position will prevail. Some have even argued that Labour has to make a stark choice — should it seek future electoral success, suggesting it needs to return to centrist policies, or should it remain true to its ideological roots, in which case it will be very hard to win elections.

Using the source, evaluate the view that the Labour Party has returned to its original ideological position.

(30 marks)

In your response you must:

- *compare the different opinions in the source*
- *consider this view and the alternative to this view in a balanced way*
- *use knowledge and understanding to help you analyse and evaluate*

ⓔ In your answer you need to establish at the outset what the original ideological position of Labour actually was. It is probably easiest to use the socialist roots of Labour, especially from the 1940s period, although it would be valid to describe 'Blairism' as fundamental. Indeed both could be used. You then need to describe the current position of Labour, at the time of writing, and compare it with its ideological roots. You should refer to material from the socialist section of the political ideas part of the course in illustrating your answer. An overall evaluation is then needed.

Student A

The source suggests two different views of the Corbyn revolution. One is that it is a fundamental return to the roots of socialism in Britain. The other is that it is just a temporary blip and that Labour is still a social democratic party that does not conform to socialist principles. **a**

The Labour Party that introduced the traditional policies supported such policies as these: the nationalisation of major industries such as coal, rail and steel, the redistribution of wealth through taxation and welfare, a strong and completely free welfare state and the widening of opportunities for all people no matter what their background. It was these policies that were pursued in the 1940s and to some extent in the 1970s. Old Labour, as it was known, also supported powerful trade unions to protect the interests of workers against the greed of capitalist employers. **b**

Jeremy Corbyn became Labour leader after Ed Miliband stood down in 2015. This was because many members of the party and many new members all believed that Labour had moved away from its traditional role of protecting the working classes. In fact they believed that Labour had betrayed the working class by encouraging capitalism and by not dealing with inequalities in living standards. The problem is, however, that most Labour voters and most Labour MPs do not support these left-wing socialist ideas.

What the moderate Blairites argue is that Old Labour is really a thing of the past and that New Labour is in fact the heart of the party. So they do support poverty relief and the protection of the welfare state, but New Labour also encourages capitalism and does not accept that workers need strong trade unions any more. New Labour also believes that wealth creators should be allowed to keep most of their wealth and not be subject to very high taxes. In other words, inequality in society is acceptable as long as it means extra wealth is created. New Labour also stresses equality of opportunity largely through a strong and fair education system. Tony Blair said the answer to Britain's problems was 'education, education, education'. **c**

The most important aspect of this question concerns clause 4 of the Labour Party constitution. This concerned the bringing of the economic resources of the country into public ownership and stated that the fruits of industry should be shared out equally. This is the most basic socialist principle. It was repealed by New Labour in 1994 when Blair defeated the left of the party. Obviously this was an abandonment of a cherished part of socialist history in Britain so it was very significant. What is not clear is whether the Corbynite wing of the party which is now in charge would restore the principles of clause 4. **d**

The answer to this question is therefore, as the source says, that Labour certainly has returned to its roots, if we believe its roots consist of left-wing socialism. However, also as the source says, if we think that Labour's roots are exemplified by Blairism and New Labour, then we can say that Labour has moved away from these in a left direction. **e**

e **15/30 marks awarded.** This is a rather disorganised answer. It also mostly ignores the source. **a** The introduction gives a clue that this is not going to be a very coherent answer. It is never clear what the student means by basic principles and how he or she is going to compare modern Labour ideas to these principles. **b** There is a useful account of basic Labour principles but this is very partial — it is still not clear what the basic principles actually are. **c** Dealing with the split in Labour under Corbyn is difficult, but this account is not very coherent. It does contain one very lucid passage **d** but this is not typical. **e** There is some clarity in the short conclusion, but this is not a reflection of the answer as a whole. Overall, this limited answer demonstrates the importance of developing a coherent plan and sticking to it.

e AO1: 6/10 marks, AO2: 5/10 marks, AO3: 4/10 marks

Student B

There is a great deal of controversy over what Labour's original ideological position is. If we look at Labour in the long term we are looking at some form of socialism, but if we treat Labour as really 'New Labour' the picture is very different. The source also asks the question of whether the current policies of the party are permanent or whether they will change when Corbyn eventually loses power. Both of these questions will be explored in this answer. **a**

Although the Labour Party had its origins in trade unionism and pure socialism, most would argue that genuine Labour principles were developed in the 1940s under Attlee and his associates such as Bevan and Morrison. It is also the party of such socialist thinkers as Crosland and Foot and Benn. Their principles revolved around the welfare state, the public ownership of major industries, the redistribution of income and support for strong trade unions. This was not pure socialism but it was a slightly moderated British version of it. **b** When we consider what Blair and New Labour did we find that some of this form of socialism was retained and some of it was abandoned. Blair repealed clause 4 which meant he did not intend to pursue nationalisation and that he accepted that there would be some inequality. New Labour followed the Rawls principles **b** that inequality can be justified as long as it creates wealth and as long as it is not at the expense of the least well off in society. New Labour did not restore union power but certainly did support and extend the welfare state. The party also promoted education for equality of opportunity and introduced an extensive anti-poverty programme. However, most commentators agreed that the party moved away from socialism because it accepted capitalism and refused to modify it significantly. Blair and co were no longer interested in class conflict. **b**

Turning to the leftward swing of the party after 2015 when it had suffered two election defeats, and failed to win again in 2017, there is no doubt that the party was returning to some of its 1940s roots, what the source calls British socialism. **c** The Corbynites have supported the nationalisation of rail and some other industries, want to restore trade union power and want to introduce a steeply progressive tax system to redistribute income. They also strongly support an extensive and well-funded welfare state. They perhaps do not go as far as the former socialists in the party but it is very much a step back as the source suggests.

Of course if we see Labour principles as those of New Labour, a moderate form of social democracy, we come to a very different conclusion. **d** The left shift of the party is well away from these principles. It is a move towards a more collectivist society and one where the balance of power should shift away from capitalism and towards the working classes. A good example is their opposition to zero hours contracts and a gig economy. New Labour and its current supporters are much less opposed. All agree on a generous minimum wage but there are large differences on how progressive the tax system should be. It is therefore clear that there has been a marked change in the principles of the party once again. As the source mentions, however, the change may be a temporary one. It may be that once Corbyn has gone, Labour will once again become moderate along the lines of New Labour and the Third Way. This seems to be what most MPs want and perhaps the voters too. If that is the case the only question we need to ask is whether Labour no longer shares the principles of the party before the 1990s. d

In conclusion we should repeat that Labour came a long way from its roots in the 1990s. Clause 4 was abandoned and the idea of class conflict rejected. The party espoused individualism and private enterprise and accepted the limited role of the state in capitalism. It did continue to support a strong welfare state on Beveridge principles and still seeks to reduce poverty and inequality but not to the extent of calling itself a socialist party. Whether Labour is going to return to those ideological roots depends on how well Corbyn and his supporters can maintain control of the party. e

e **27/30 marks awarded.** This is a very well-organised and argued answer. Its only small weakness is that it does not develop any of its main points quite fully enough and its analysis and evaluation are slightly limited. But these are very minor criticisms and they result in a loss of only 1 mark for each assessment objective.

a The introduction is strong and clear. We know how this student intends to address the question. There are frequent and relevant references to the source material, including comments on different views in the source. b The student also makes good use of knowledge of the political ideas part of the course, showing good awareness of different conceptions of socialism and social democracy, including reference to leading thinkers. c Knowledge is always up to date and the student makes good comparisons with the past. These evaluations are made extremely and directly relevant to the actual question being posed. d The quality of those evaluations is also excellent throughout. e The final conclusion is especially strong. It summarises the analysis well and reflects accurately the body of the answer.

e **AO1: 9/10 marks, AO2: 9/10 marks, AO3: 9/10 marks**

Question 2

Evaluate the statement that 'all the main political parties in the UK are fundamentally liberal parties'.

(30 marks)

You must consider this view and the alternative to this view in a balanced way.

e Your introduction should explain the term 'liberal' ideas. Having done this, your answer should evaluate the extent to which the current political stance of the three main parties includes these principles. Do not look at smaller parties, though the SNP might be included in view of its successes since 2010. The issue of whether they should be described as fundamentally 'liberal' should constitute the concluding part of your answer.

Student A

Before we consider this question it is necessary to establish what is meant by 'liberal'. [a] I assume that liberal means a strong sense of protection of human rights, a belief in a democratic political system, widespread freedom and equality for all individuals and minority groups. Liberals also support equality and limited government. We can now examine how much the three main parties, Labour, Conservatives and even Liberal Democrats, are genuinely liberal. [b]

The Conservative Party is probably the least liberal of the parties although Theresa May, when she took over in 2016, said that she wanted to treat all people as equal. It is also true that the Conservatives protect human rights, although they have promised to repeal the HRA and replace it with a British Bill of Rights. It is also true that they accept the rule of law although there may be a suspicion that they would like to take more extreme anti-liberal steps in the interests of national security. [c]

The Labour Party has always been close to liberal parties. Labour believes in the equality of all and also believes in a strong democracy. Labour passed the Equality Act which makes sure that no groups in society, including women, are discriminated against. Labour also supports the idea of liberty, although in the past the party has sacrificed some liberty in the interests of socialist measures. [d] Labour is a very democratic party and it is also now very internally democratic. The way it elects its leader, with everyone having a vote, is very democratic even though it has caused great trouble as Jeremy Corbyn was elected against the will of the party's MPs. Social justice is something that liberals and social democrats agree upon. This means that society should be organised so that no people have excessive advantages over others. This is a view expressed by the philosopher John Rawls [e] who coined the difference principle which says that the rich should not prosper at the expense of the poor.

Turning to the Liberal Democrats themselves it is clear they are a liberal party. They support strong protection of human rights in Britain and hope to reform the constitution so that it is more democratic. They also believe strongly in human rights and want to entrench them even further. Therefore they support higher taxes for the wealthy and lower taxes for low-income groups. They also wish to promote equality for women and minority groups. Above all, members of the party support tolerance and they believe in a multicultural society and free movement of people.

All major parties in the UK are basically liberal. This is because liberalism is entrenched in British society, and there is a deep sense of tolerance, democracy, rights, fairness and a love of liberty. It follows then that all parties should follow these values. They are under threat from other parties such as UKIP, but it seems likely that Britain will continue to be a liberal political system. [f]

@ **14/30 marks awarded.** This is a reasonable answer in terms of explaining the positive view that all main parties are fundamentally liberal. [a] It starts well with a statement of liberal principles and a description of where the essay is going. [b] However, the answer then develops two serious faults. One is that it is not thorough enough in its explanations of its analysis. This is clearly seen at **c** and **d** where an interesting and relevant theme is introduced but not explained properly. Similarly, at **e** the student introduces some modern liberal theory — of Rawls. This is taken from the political ideas part of the course and it is generally very good practice to do this, but unfortunately it is undeveloped. The second fault, exemplified by a limited conclusion, is that this is a very one-sided response. **f** The rubric states that your answer should include a counter view to the question in a balanced way. This is not done here. The ways in which parties are not liberal are sparse and very limited.

e A01: 6/10 marks, A02: 4/10 marks, A03: 4/10 marks

Student B

We cannot consider this question without determining what liberal principles we are talking about. If we take the liberal principles as expressed by such key liberal thinkers as Locke, Mill, Beveridge and Rawls we have an idea of what these principles are. Locke was interested in democracy and government by consent so that is a critical value. Mill added a stress on individual liberty and limited government. Beveridge believed in welfare and the idea that society has a responsibility to care for those unable to care for themselves. Finally, Rawls was concerned with social justice and reducing inequalities. **a** We can now evaluate the extent to which the main parties support these liberal values and assess ways in which they may fall short of them. In other words, we can assess how liberal they really are. **b**

We should obviously begin with the Liberal Democrats. They very strongly believe in Mill's and Locke's principles of freedom and rights, and representative government which is limited and controlled by the people. This is exemplified by their strong support for democracy and constitutional reform. They seek to make the political system more decentralised and wish to introduce greater constitutional safeguards against powerful government and in the interests of protecting freedom and rights. Their desire for greater democracy is exemplified by their seeking to have an elected second chamber and to reform the electoral system. The party very strongly supports the principles of the welfare state and has more recently come round to Rawls' view that social justice is essential, even if it means state intervention. This is the only possibly illiberal aspect of the party. Some members, known as Orange Book Liberals, believe that there has been too much interference in economic life in Lib Dem policies and they wish to restore free markets, a very old classical liberal idea. However, it is no surprise that Liberal Democrats are very liberal in their outlook. **c**

Labour has a great deal in common with the Liberal Democrats. It was Labour who introduced the Human Rights Act, reformed the constitution after 1997 and passed the Equality Act. Labour believes strongly in Rawls' idea of social justice by having a strong welfare system and a progressive tax system. Labour outlaws discrimination and supports tolerance for all groups in society. Above all, Labour has supported equality of opportunity, especially through education. New Labour abandoned many socialist principles but it replaced some of them with a commitment to such equality. In a free society there may be too much inequality so Labour insists on strong education and opportunities to make it a fair society. b Having said all this, there are a few illiberal tendencies in Labour. While classical liberals are suspicious of too much state interference in the economy and society, Labour has always supported intervention and regulation to achieve its aims. It is also true that Labour is rather 'soft' on democratic reform. For example, it has not supported electoral reform to make the political system more representative. b

The Conservatives have been a neo-liberal party of course, but this is a different kind of liberalism. It represents economic freedom that classical liberals supported, but they have also been neo-conservative which supports a strong, harsh state, too strong for most liberals. On the other hand, many modern conservatives such as Cameron, Osborne and Clark have a liberal outlook. They accept there must be a degree of social justice and like Labour they support equality of opportunity. As May has said, they seek to govern for the many and not the few. This anti-elitism is very liberal in nature. However, it has to be said that the Conservatives are still willing to sacrifice civil liberties in the interests of national security. Furthermore, they have consistently opposed democratic reforms such as an elected second chamber and electoral reform. They may claim to be tolerant to all groups, but there is a suspicion that they are anti-multiculturalism and this is why they wish to curb immigration. d Turning to social justice, the party had adopted some liberal measures, such as increasing the minimum wage and reducing tax for the low paid, but it still defends the interests of the very wealthy and of business, where taxes have been reduced significantly. Finally, the Conservatives are less supportive of the welfare state than other parties. Some even argue they would prefer to abandon Beveridge's principles and privatise much of the welfare state.

So we can see that all main parties support some basic liberal principles such as tolerance, democracy and equality of opportunity but there are variations in the degree to which they support them. The Conservatives are certainly the least liberal of the parties. e

e **29/30 marks awarded.** This is an excellent essay. a It begins with a very strong introduction defining the key ideas to be explored. b It also clearly indicates that this is going to be a genuinely evaluative answer. Several sections demonstrate this technique which is required in the rubric. d The section on the Conservative Party is especially strong on evaluation. A second great strength is that it draws extensively from the political ideas part of the course — c is a good example of this. References to key liberal thinkers throughout give this answer great authority. These two virtues — evaluation and synoptic links to other parts of the course — make it worthy of almost full marks. It is also extremely well organised and has a logical structure. e The only small weakness is a weak conclusion which is valid but underdeveloped.

e **AO1: 10/10 marks, AO2: 10/10 marks, AO3: 9/10 marks**

Electoral systems

NB Students should perfect their knowledge also of the 2017 general election, but should use the same techniques as those indicated here to answer similar source-based questions on 2017.

Question 1

Study the data in the table and the commentary that follows.

Party	% votes won	% seats won	No. of seats won	Notes
The result of the UK general election, May 2015				
Conservative	36.9	50.9	331	Conservative support is concentrated in southern England
Labour	30.4	35.7	232	Labour support is concentrated in northern England.
Scottish National Party	4.7	8.6	6	In Scotland the SNP won 95% of the available seats on 50% of the Scottish vote
Liberal Democrats	7.9	1.2	8	The party's support is widely dispersed
Democratic Unionist Party	0.6	1.2	8	The DUP only contests seats in Northern Ireland
Sinn Fein	0.6	0.6	4	Northern Ireland only
Plaid Cymru	0.6	0.5	3	Contests seats in Wales
UKIP	12.6	0.2	1	UKIP support is very widely dispersed
Green Party	3.8	0.2	1	Support for the Greens is very dispersed
Others	2.5	1.0	6	Mostly in Northern Ireland

On the face of it these data suggest that there is severe discrimination against some parties and in favour of others. However, it can also be argued that, despite the fact that no party won an overall majority of the popular vote, a single party was able to form a government with a working parliamentary majority. We must also beware of declaring that first past the post always discriminates against small parties. The SNP's success is a case in point.

Using the source, evaluate the impact of first past the post in terms of representative democracy.

(30 marks)

In your response you must:

- *compare the different opinions in the source*
- *use knowledge and understanding to help you analyse and evaluate*

ⓔ The impact of first past the post can be divided into three main parts. First, the way in which it discriminates in favour of, or against, certain parties. Use data from the source to illustrate this. Second, what impact it has on voters. Third, what impact it has on the formation of government. Use the data to evaluate whether the winning party has democratic legitimacy. An overall evaluation of whether the system serves representative democracy well or badly should be deployed.

Student A

First past the post is the electoral system used for general elections in the UK. It is a system which has often been criticised for its unfairness, especially to smaller parties. The system also makes votes have unequal value and leads to a large number of wasted votes. In this essay I will evaluate the use of first past the post, stressing its advantages and disadvantages. a

The source material clearly shows the unfairness of first past the post (FPTP). The worst problem was faced by UKIP. It won 12.6% of the vote but won only one seat. This is because its support is spread evenly across the whole country. The Green Party also suffered with only one seat for 3.8% of the vote and the Liberal Democrats with eight seats for 7.9% of the votes. On the other hand, it was a huge advantage for the Conservatives. The Tories won only 36.9% of the total votes but were returned with an overall majority and 331 seats. b

Turning to votes, the system results in a large number of wasted votes. Wasted votes are those for small parties which have no chance of winning seats. Votes are also wasted in safe seats where only one party has any chance of winning. On the other hand, votes in marginal seats are worth much more as are votes for the larger parties. c Turning to the SNP we can see that it won virtually all the seats in Scotland even though it only won half of the votes there. This is because its support in Scotland is very concentrated. This is also why Labour and the Conservatives do relatively well.

This is in contrast to proportional systems where every vote counts and the various parties are treated more fairly. The regional list system is the fairest as far as parties are concerned.

First past the post has a number of advantages. It is a simple system which people understand and produces a quick result. People rejected an alternative system in a referendum in 2011. It also creates a strong connection between constituencies and their MP because there is only one MP (unlike STV where there are six). In some list systems there are no constituencies at all. d Above all though FPTP means that one party usually wins the election and there is a decisive result. This avoids all the problems of minority governments and coalitions and unstable governments as we see in places like Italy. e

In all elections in the UK apart from 2010 there has been a government with a parliamentary majority and very often the majority has been very large. Governments with a large majority can get all their legislation through and so government is far more efficient.

So we can see that FPTP has a number of drawbacks as far as the voters are concerned and discriminates against smaller parties, but we can also see that it is a better system when it comes to strong and stable government. In summary therefore it is a balanced argument and it depends what you want from an electoral system. f

e **15/30 marks awarded.** This answer is structured well and addresses parts of the question, but it also has several fundamental faults. a The introduction would normally be satisfactory, but it does not address the exact question which is asking about representative democracy. In fact this is a general weakness of this answer — its failure to address the wording of the question. b There is some effective reference to the source, but there is not enough of it and it does not address the substance of the data which measure the relative value of votes. c The section on marginal and safe seats is accurate but does not relate the answer to

representative democracy (i.e. are voters in safe seats effectively represented?)
d, e Parts of the answer are not really related to the question as they are discussing advantages and disadvantages without relating them to representative democracy.
f The conclusion tries to summarise, but again does not address the question. There is also no assessment of how the information in the data comes to a different conclusion from the written section of the source.

e A01: 6/10 marks, A02: 4/10 marks, A03: 5/10 marks

Student B

The question refers to representative democracy. The UK is a representative democracy which means that the system should ensure that people are fully represented by individuals and parties. This means that their interests are taken into consideration and are protected if they are in danger. It also means fair representation, that everyone and every party has an equal influence in the system. Many critics have suggested that the electoral system (FPTP) does not serve representative democracy well. In particular, it makes votes have unequal value and discriminates unfairly against some parties and in favour of others. This essay will examine the arguments and assess whether they are valid, using the data and information shown in the source. **a**

The source data show that votes are of unequal value. It takes many more votes to elect a Green candidate, a Liberal Democrat and, most seriously, a UKIP member than it does to elect a Labour or Conservative member. As for the SNP it has a huge advantage with nearly all the seats in Scotland on only 50% of the vote in that country. **b**

The really serious problem here is that the two main parties are hugely over-represented and the extent of their support is over-exaggerated by the system. It also means that many millions of people are not really represented at all. The millions of UKIP voters have only one MP to represent all of them in parliament. On the other hand, the Scots are over-represented in parliament and the SNP has more influence than its support warrants.

The data do not show that there are too many safe seats in the UK. Safe seats are those that can only be won by one party or another. It means that the constituents there may not be well represented as the MPs are not really accountable to the electorate. **c** Those who represent marginal seats, on the other hand, are more accountable because they will have to fight to retain their seat at the next election.

Turning to the broader question raised in the written part of the source **d** we can see that the system is good for representative democracy because it produces governments with a clear majority and this means they have a clear mandate to govern. Coalition governments, which might result from a proportional electoral system, do not have a proper mandate and so are less representative. However, there is a great downside to this characteristic. No government since 1945 has ever won a majority of all the votes cast. In 2005 Labour was elected with only 35% of the national vote. In 2015 the figure was not much better at 36.9%. This raises the question of whether the government is truly representative. The system also weakens opposition because the small parties do not gain fair representation. We can therefore ask the question of whether the government is properly accountable. Of course, opponents of this view will argue that the alternative is a chaotic system where small parties will hold the balance of power and have too much influence. Before the 2015 election there was a fear that a Labour government might have to depend on the support of the Scottish Nationalists who would demand independence as the price of their cooperation. This would distort representation. **e**

In conclusion we can see that there are advantages and disadvantages of FPTP in terms of representative democracy. In the end there is a strong case either way and the source expresses this. It really depends on what kind of representative democracy we want to see in the UK. **f**

e 27/30 marks awarded. This is a very strong answer. Its great strength is that it constantly refers directly to the question and addresses it. It has two small weaknesses. The first is that it does not use the statistical data fully enough. The second is that its conclusion is rather weak and indecisive.

a The introduction is excellent, making it clear how the answer is going to address the question and defining representative democracy. **b** The second paragraph is an example of the lack in the use of the statistical data. **c** The answer shows a good technique in demonstrating relevant information not shown in the source and how valuable it would be. Another strength of this answer is that it engages with all the source and this is demonstrated at **d**. **e** There is also some good historical context. Information about historical change is always useful and adds to AO1 marks. **f** Unfortunately the conclusion is indecisive.

e AO1: 9/10 marks, AO2: 9/10 marks, AO3: 9/10 marks

Question 2

Evaluate the use of referendums in the UK. (30 marks)

e Your introduction should define referendums and explain when they have been used, together with a general statement of why they have become controversial. You should evaluate this question by looking at the advantages and disadvantages of referendums. Your answer should be full of examples from recent referendums. In your conclusion you could suggest the circumstances when referendums might be appropriate and when they might not be.

Student A

A referendum is a vote held to determine an important political issue. It is a reality of referendums that the question has to be yes or no. There can be no other answer. The verdict of referendums has to be compulsory even though parliament is sovereign. It is unimaginable that parliament would overturn a referendum. The most important recent referendum was in 2016 over the UK's membership of the European Union when a majority decided we should leave. There have also been many other referendums which will be described in this essay. **a**

There are a number of reasons why referendums are desirable. The first is that they settle an issue once and for all. When there is major controversy it can disrupt the political system for a long time. A second reason is that the government itself might be divided on an issue so a referendum can end the uncertainty. This was long the case with the Conservatives who have been divided over the EU. Third, referendums represent the purest form of democracy. It is the verdict of the people and in the end, in a democracy, the people are sovereign. Finally, a referendum secures the consent of the people in a way that parliament and government cannot. So we can see that there are several good reasons for holding referendums. **b**

On the other hand, there are also several drawbacks to referendum use. First, there is the tyranny of the majority. This means that the majority who vote one way are forcing the minority into a decision with which they do not agree. This is, however, unavoidable because there has to be a majority and a minority. **c** Second, referendums undermine representative democracy so there is a danger that the people will no longer respect parties, government and parliament if they become used to making their own decisions. A third problem with referendums is that the people may not understand the issue well enough. They may also be fed dubious information and opinion, as occurred during the EU referendum. Elected representatives are more likely to be moderate in their opinions and try to find compromises. **b**

In general, referendums can be very divisive. They split the nation and they reveal how divided we can be. Elected politicians can unite the nation but referendums tend to do the opposite.

We have had several referendums in recent years. The EU referendum was in many ways a problem because it has caused more controversy than it has solved. The Scots believe they have been forced to leave the EU against their wishes. The same is true of London which voted to stay in the EU. In contrast, however, the Scottish referendum did solve an issue which was threatening the unity of the UK. There was a referendum in 2011 over whether to change the electoral system to AV. There was a very decisive rejection which was clear enough but it has to be pointed out that many people used it as a vote against the Liberal Democrats who had broken their promise over tuition fees when they were in coalition with the Conservatives. So we do not really know what the population thought about a new system. It was, incidentally, a very difficult issue for ordinary people to understand. **d**

It is a very balanced argument whether referendums are a good thing or not. It is very difficult to evaluate the issue. The answer is probably that it depends on the issue. Some issues are suitable for a referendum and others are less so and should be determined by government and parliament. **e**

e **17/30 marks awarded.** In some ways this is a solid answer. It describes four positive aspects of referendums and four disadvantages. However, it contains a number of problems. **a** The introduction defines referendums well enough but then does not place the question in context (an ideal context would be the controversies surrounding the EU referendum). Some examples are added at the end but would be so much better used if they directly illustrated the four advantages and four disadvantages of referendums as described in **b**. **c** The issue of Scotland and the EU vote would be a perfect opportunity for this approach. **d** When the examples are included, the descriptions are not fully developed and are limited in scope. A few other examples should be added, for example the devolution votes in 1997 or local votes on congestion charges. **e** Finally, the conclusion is weak. It is an interesting conclusion to reach — it depends on what the referendum is about — but the student does not illustrate this point with specific examples. Introductions and conclusions should be as fully developed as any other part of a long answer.

e **AO1: 6/10 marks, AO2: 6/10 marks, AO3: 5/10 marks**

Student B

Referendums are votes held to resolve an important political or constitutional issue. These normally concern proposed changes to how we are governed or to how we are taxed. Two recent referendums, of course, on Scottish independence and EU membership, have been about very fundamental issues which is why the voice of the people was needed. Referendums, though, are highly controversial. Are they as democratic as we believe? Are they preferable to decisions made by an accountable government? Do people understand issues well enough? There are many questions to be asked like this. This essay will describe the key issues and try to find some conclusions. **a**

The great attraction of a referendum is that it is the pure voice of the people, the purest form of democracy as favourably described by Plato in ancient Greece. **b** The people are really sovereign in a democracy, so surely it is they who should make such decisions? The referendum on Scottish independence is the most important example of this. Who else should decide the future of the Scottish people but the Scottish people? The Scots would probably not have accepted a decision if independence had been forced on them! As it happens it was rejected so the issue was settled, at least until the outcome of the EU referendum re-opened the controversy.

Referendums can also resolve issues which divide the government and the people. The Scottish vote was also an example of this, but so too was the EU referendum. The Conservative Party and the whole nation were divided about Europe and had been for many years so this was an opportunity to deal with the problem. However, as we will see, it perhaps was a failure because it only divided the nation further rather than uniting it.

A third claim made for referendums is that the people will respect and consent to decisions they have made themselves. There is a great deal of disillusionment with politics and politicians at this time so referendums give us decisions which will not be disputed. The 2011 vote on changing the electoral system is a good example. Would the people have respected a new electoral system imposed on them by politicians, especially unpopular ones?

So, we can see that there are a number of good reasons for using referendums, but they also have their problems. The main problem is that they create a majority which might be seen to be dictating to a minority. This was best seen in 2016 when Scotland was unwillingly being dragged out of the EU against its will. The same was true of London. It all hinged on deciding whether the UK is indeed one single nation. **c** Politicians, on the other hand, can find compromises between the majority and minorities. However, this was perhaps not possible in the case of the Scottish and EU referendums where there was a straight yes or no / leave or remain. **c**

We can turn to the problem that many people do not understand the issues. This was a major criticism of the EU and the AV referendums. It was also true that the people were subjected to a large amount of half truths and sometimes simple misinformation. Elected politicians are not likely to suffer from this problem.

There are also a number of smaller issues. What happens, for example, if the turnout is very low, as happens with votes on local congestion charges. Are such referendums democratically valid? Also, what if the outcome is very close? This happened over Welsh devolution in 1997 when there was 1% between the two sides and the EU vote when the gap was 4%. Is such a tiny majority a good enough reason to make a major change? Finally, we can point to the influence of the tabloids and their appeals to people's emotions rather than their reason. **d**

In conclusion, any evaluation is difficult to make because there are balanced arguments in favour and against referendum use. To some extent it may depend on the issues. Scottish independence calls demanded a referendum, but was it necessary for a change to electoral reform? However, there is one compelling argument that works against the future use of referendums except in certain particular circumstances. This is that referendums tend to divide communities whereas the main aim of democratic politics is to unite the community. This was strongly illustrated by the EU vote. **e**

e **30/30 marks awarded.** This is a very strong answer worthy of full marks. It is well constructed, with a good introduction and decisive conclusion, and a logical pattern of points with plenty of well-applied examples. **a** The introduction describes referendums and when they have been used and then puts the question in context, explaining why it is important today. **b** There is a small error in that Plato actually criticised this form of democracy, but positive marking means that all the good points of this answer outweigh such a minor problem. **c** The greatest strengths of this essay are its evaluation and use of examples. **d** A good technique used here is to add several minor points at the end without spending excessive time explaining them. This broadens the whole evaluation. **e** Finally, there is a very good, firm conclusion which summarises the evaluation but comes up with a decisive conclusion that one side outweighs the other.

e AO1: 10/10 marks, AO2: 10/10 marks, AO3: 10/10 marks

Voting behaviour and the media

Question 1

Study the two tables of data and the commentary that follows.

Class DE voting for Labour

Election year	% class DE voting Labour
1964	64
1987	53
1997	59
2010	40
2015	41
2017	59

Source: Ipsos MORI/Earlham Sociology

Class AB voting for the Conservatives

Election year	% class AB voting Conservative
1964	78
1987	57
1997	59
2010	40
2015	45
2017	43

Source: Ipsos MORI/Earlham Sociology

It used to be said that long-term voting behaviour could always be explained by social class. Certainly the early data, going back to the 1960s, suggested this. However, two factors are disturbing this belief. First, other demographic factors are becoming important, and second, many more voters are becoming volatile and unpredictable in their voting habits.

Using the source, evaluate the importance of class in voting behaviour.　　(30 marks)

In your response you must:
- *compare the different opinions in the source*
- *use knowledge and understanding to help you analyse and evaluate*

ⓔ The sources show that social class used to be important but appears to be becoming less so. This should be described at the outset and data from the sources quoted. You then need to offer explanations of, first, why class appears to be becoming less significant and, second, what factors may have replaced class in explaining voting behaviour. You also need to attempt an overall evaluation of how important class remains today.

Student A

Class used to be the main determinant of voting behaviour but this has reduced in recent times and there are now many other ways in which we can predict how people will vote. In particular this essay will look at factors such as age, gender, ethnicity and income levels. Class is still important and can perhaps explain about 50% of voting behaviour, but the question is how we can explain the other 40–50%. This essay will also look at why people are so much more volatile in their voting habits. ⓐ

Obviously class is very important. The source says that about 59% of the working class voted Labour in 2017 and 43% of the middle class voted Conservative. This compares with about 80% of the middle classes supporting the Conservatives in the 1960s and about 64% of the working class voting Labour, so class is important but nowhere near as important as it used to be. Let us now look at other demographic factors. ⓑ

There is a very big correlation between age and support for the parties. In 2017 the 18–24 age group supported Labour in much greater numbers than the Conservatives, 67% against 18%. As people get older, however, they become increasingly Conservative in their outlook and voting. If we look at the over 65 age group we see that twice as many of this group voted Conservative as voted Labour. When we look at the EU referendum we find that the age factor is even more marked with most over 65s voting to leave. **c** The same was true of the Scottish independence vote in 2014 where most older people voted against independence and the young, especially the very young, tended to vote for independence. **c**

Gender tells us little. The evidence for some time has been that men and women divide their votes about equally between the two parties. This is also true of voting for the Liberal Democrats which is 50-50. So we can ignore gender as being insignificant.

Ethnicity is important. The vast majority of black and Asian voters support Labour. In 2017 two thirds of this group voted Labour while only a quarter voted Conservative. However, the number supporting each party is falling so it is declining as a factor. Increasingly, Sikhs and Hindus are supporting the Conservatives.

Income is another important factor. In particular those on lower incomes are major supporters of UKIP and of Brexit. Higher income groups tend to reject UKIP and mostly voted to remain in the EU. Income is not quite the same as class as there is a weaker correlation between income and parties than can be seen in the classes. **d**

An increasing number of voters are becoming unpredictable. This is because they are swing voters who make their decisions based on specific factors such as the policies of the parties (rational choice model). Some also take into account the image of the parties and party leaders. They may, for example, not trust a party to handle the economy well.

So, if we ask whether class is helpful in explaining voting behaviour, we have to say yes it is, but with two exceptions. The first is that other factors such as age and ethnicity are also important. The other is that class is declining in importance. While it was crucial in the 1960s it is now only a rough guide to voting intentions. **e**

e **18/30 marks awarded.** **a** There is quite a good introduction which makes it clear how the essay will be organised and addresses the question broadly. **b** The student refers to the source in the second paragraph, but this is rather brief and incomplete. It is important to engage fully with the source. **c** There is a reasonable section on age, although again this could be more thorough. **d** From then on the answer becomes generalised and there are few data or facts to underpin the arguments made. It is important to use as much specific evidence as possible. **e** The conclusion does address the question but does not really fully engage with it and does not evaluate successfully, estimating which factors are more important than others.

e **AO1: 5/10 marks, AO2: 6/10 marks, AO3: 7/10 marks**

Student B

In the 1960s political scientists saw class as the most important factor in voting behaviour and so they concentrated on the minority who did not vote with their class identity. The source clearly shows this strong correlation. But that was back in the 1960s, the situation has now changed. It has changed in several ways — class is less an indicator of voting behaviour than it was. The source shows this change with working-class Labour voting falling from 64% to 41% and middle-class Tory voting going down from 78% to 45% by 2015. Even though working class Labour support grew again in 2017, it remains true that the link between class and party support remains relatively weak. Second, there are other demographic factors such as age, region and ethnicity that have become important. Finally, there are other new theories of voting behaviour such as rational choice, economic and instrumental voting which are becoming more important than class. The source says that this leads to unpredictable voting and volatile voting with voters changing from one party to another between elections. This undermines our understanding of the effect of demographic factors. a

There has also been a process known as class dealignment. Fewer people associate themselves with their class and so their voting becomes less predictable.

If we look at the 2016 EU referendum people voted unpredictably in terms of class. The working classes mostly voted Leave which was a policy of the right-wing UKIP party and the right wing of the Conservatives. Class does tell us something about voting for small parties, with class AB voters tending to support the Greens and Liberal Democrats. The working class DE heavily support UKIP. So we can now see that class is less important than it used to be in terms of voting habits b but it remains an important factor in some regards.

If we look at other demographic factors we can see that they have become just as important as class in predicting voting. Beginning with age there is a very strong link between age and voting. People over 65 are more likely to vote for the Conservative Party. Nearly half of the over 65 age group voted Conservative compared with only 23% for Labour. Very few young voters support the Liberal Democrats who are heavily supported by the middle aged. We can therefore say that age is as good a predictor of voting behaviour as social class because the correlation figures are very similar. c

Ethnicity is an even better indicator. The vast majority of BME voters support Labour. This is a declining number, however. In 2017, 65% of BME voters voted Labour compared to 70% in 1997. The source does not really tell the full story here. This is because some factors are affecting other factors. So, the south is mostly Conservative but this is likely to be because incomes are usually higher in the south, so it is income, not region that is at work. Similarly, BME people are more likely to have low incomes and so will support Labour but not UKIP for obvious reasons. Again it is class and income at work here, not ethnicity. d

Recent elections showed very marked regional variations in voting. London, for example, broke the general trend and a majority supported Labour. The same is true of most, but not all, of the north where UKIP used to do well. Conversely, the south of England was solidly Conservative. Region has become extremely important, rivalling class as a factor. Generally Labour is stronger in cities than in small towns and the countryside.

The source refers to non-demographic factors. **e** Increasingly voters are proving volatile and many are floating voters. This means they look at each election separately. Economic performance and trust is a key issue, meaning the image of the parties and their leader as being economically responsible. The Labour defeat in 2015 was considerably to do with the fact that the party was seen as divided, irresponsible with the economy and poorly led by Ed Miliband. Much of the research suggests this was true.

Rational voting is also important. This is where voters look at party policies and decide which is the best for them. It may well be, therefore, that in both 2010 and 2015 large numbers of voters were attracted to the Conservatives because they promised tax cuts and to UKIP with the prospect of a referendum on EU membership and reductions in immigration which was a major issue in 2015.

One factor that appears to tell us virtually nothing is gender because men and women show the same voting patterns.

In summary, therefore, class remains useful in explaining voting behaviour, though far from as useful as it was decades ago. The majority of voters still vote the way we would expect given their occupation and income. However, there is no doubt that other demographic factors give us strong clues as to voting behaviour. Finally, we must remember that a growing number of voters do not conform to these factors and instead judge each party on their merits and examine policies carefully. The source shows a clear correlation between class and voting, but then accepts that other factors may now be more important. This is a valid analysis. **j**

e **29/30 marks awarded.** The great strength of this answer is that it engages with the source material. In this case, the essay's conclusion agrees with the analysis in the source and the student has explained why in the body of the essay.

a, **b** There is very good use of data. There is a slightly weaker section at **c** when the answer becomes a little too generalised. There is a very strong engagement with the evidence at **d** when conventional data are challenged. This is good technique. **e** It is also good technique to refer to the source material at various opportunities. **j** The conclusion is meaningful, summarises the analysis and again engages with the source.

e **AO1: 9/10 marks, AO2: 10/10 marks, AO3: 10/10 marks**

Question 2

Evaluate the relative importance of different demographic factors in voting behaviour.

(30 marks)

e At the beginning you need to establish which demographic factors you are going to examine. You should only attempt a question like this if you have command of some key data to use as evidence. Vague generalisations will gain some credit, but not as much as hard data. Using data as evidence, you need to identify which factors are more important than others. You should then attempt an overall evaluation of what the most decisive factors are.

Student A

In this essay I will be looking at a variety of demographic factors including social class, age, gender, ethnicity and region. There is no doubt that class remains the most important factor, but some of the other factors are important too. The only factor that has little importance is gender because men and women pretty much vote in the same way. There is no difference between them. First I will look at class. **a**

Class used to be the most important factor with two thirds of the working class supporting Labour and even more of the middle class supporting the Conservatives. Now, however, class is less important. There are many more 'deviant voters' who do not vote the way their class suggests they would. Only about 40% of people vote the way their class would suggest.

There is now a case for saying that age is the key factor. The young are much more likely to support Labour as well as the Greens and the Liberal Democrats and the SNP in Scotland. On the other hand, older people have become increasingly Conservative in their outlook. The over 65 age group vote Conservative by a majority of three quarters to one quarter. **b** It was always true that older people are more conservative, but now it is very marked indeed. It is also true that older people are much more likely to vote for UKIP.

Region is very important. In places like London and the northeast of England Labour is well ahead whereas in the south and the southwest (where the Conservatives won all 15 Liberal Democrat seats) the Tories are dominant. In Scotland, of course, the SNP swept the board and are very dominant. The other three main parties lost nearly all their seats in Scotland. So if we are looking for the best indication of how people will vote, class and region are the most important and almost equal in importance. **c**

Having said all this, the best indicator of how people will vote is their ethnic identity. Black and Asian British voters are far more likely to support Labour than the Conservatives. The only group that is different are Muslims whose voting is mixed between the main parties.

It is therefore clear that class remains a key factor, but it is not as important as ethnicity and it is now closely rivalled by region as a factor. One of the reasons for this is class dealignment. Fewer and fewer people identify themselves with one class or another. This means that the link between class and voting is getting weaker. **d**

e **15/30 marks awarded.** This is a reasonable essay with a good structure and coverage of the main issues. It suffers from the problem of being somewhat out of date, using 2015 figures rather than 2017. **a** The introduction promises a well-constructed answer. However, it has one major weakness and one lesser weakness. The major weakness is its lack of hard statistics as evidence. The statements made are broadly accurate but are too generalised. **b** and **c** both lack hard data. The other weakness is that there is no mention of referendums. The demographic factors in the Scottish and EU referendums were especially interesting and informative. **d** The conclusion is fine, though the material on class dealignment should be in the body of the answer.

e AO1: 4/10 marks, AO2: 5/10 marks, AO3: 6/10 marks

Student B

Back in the 1960s it was said with great justification that social class was by far the most important indicator of how a person would vote. There was the phenomenon of the 'working-class Tory voter', also called deviant voters, but still 65% of the working class voted Labour in the 1960s. Class was more important in society at that time. The working class was very distinct, as was the middle class. About 75% of the middle class voted Conservative. Furthermore, the turnout among the middle classes was higher so the Conservative disadvantage was reduced, given that the working class was larger than the middle class in the 1960s. As we shall see, class has become far less important in today's world and other demographic factors have grown in significance. This essay will examine these changes and evaluate their importance. a

Class is no longer as dominant as it used to be in most circumstances, although in some cases class still plays a big part in voting. In 2010 and 2015 the middle class (class AB) voted Tory in 40% and 45% proportion respectively. In the same elections working-class support for Labour was about 40%. So there is a correlation, but it is much weaker than it was 50 years ago. When we look at small parties, 17% of the working class voted UKIP but only 5% voted Liberal Democrat. There was clear converse support for the Lib Dems among class AB. Turning to the EU referendum there was a large middle-class bias for Remain (57%) and a working-class bias for Leave (64%). b So class remains important in circumstances other than a general election. In 2017 the picture did change a little, however, with 59% of working class voters supporting Labour — a big increase over 2015.

Gender is not an important factor. Men and women divide their vote between the parties almost in the same proportion as the whole population. Therefore this tells us nothing about voting behaviour and can be discounted.

The same cannot be said for ethnicity. Taking BME (black and ethnic minorities) as our factor, we will see that there is a very great bias towards Labour. In 2015 65% of the BME voters supported Labour (though this number has fallen by 10% since 1997). Only 23% of this community voted Conservative.

We can now turn to age and region, both of which rival class in predicting voting behaviour. With age there is a startling result from the Scottish independence referendum: 71% of the new 16- and 17-year-old voters supported independence, while only 27% of the over 65s agreed with them. The young also tend to support more radical parties such as the Greens and the SNP while the over 65s remain conservative in their outlook. In the 2015 general election only 27% of the 18–24 group voted Conservative compared to 43% for the Labour Party. In the over 65 group the outcome was almost the exact opposite of this. c

Britain has always had big regional variations in voting, with the north being mostly Labour and the south Conservative. With the exception of London, the south remains solidly Conservative and this was even more pronounced in 2015 (though it fell back slightly in 2017) when the Conservatives captured all the

Liberal Democrat seats. UKIP does well in the north of England in terms of votes, untill its collapse in 2017 though this is probably a class rather than a regional factor. [d] Of course Scotland is the most dramatic example of regional bias, with half the votes there in 2015 going to the SNP. SNP support dipped in 2017 so it remains difficult to establish how permanent this regional bias will be. The same happened in the 2016 Scottish parliamentary election.

We therefore have a great deal of conflicting evidence. We can definitely say that class remains important though its significance is in decline, gender tells us nothing, ethnicity is crucial (except among Hindu origin people who are balanced) and region has become exceptionally important. However, demographic factors are constantly changing so it is difficult to be too dogmatic. [e]

e 30/30 marks awarded. This is a very strong answer deserving of full marks. It brings the information reasonably up to date, which is important. [a] There is an excellent introduction which sets the scene, followed by a well-structured answer. [b], [c] The greatest strength of this answer is the wealth of specific statistics which are quoted as evidence. There are no generalisations unsupported by data. There is also some very good original evaluation, such as is found at [d]. [e] The conclusion is a good summary of the content of the evaluation and contains an interesting observation about historical change.

e AO1: 10/10 marks, AO2: 10/10 marks, AO3: 10/10 marks

Knowledge check answers

1 ■ Age UK is the most important pressure group representing the elderly.
- Members of the Welsh Assembly are called Assembly Members (AMs).
- People elected to local government are called local councillors.
- The 2011 referendum asked whether the UK should adopt the alternative vote (AV) system for general elections.

2 ■ In UK general elections turnout has been steadily falling with a slight recovery in 2010, 2015 and 2017.
- Turnout at referendums tends to vary greatly but it is more predictable for general elections.
- Yes. At these elections turnout tended to be a little higher.

3 People participate in several ways:
- voting at elections
- joining a political party
- being active in a pressure group
- taking part in a protest
- signing a petition or e-petition
- joining an online political campaign

4 The groups are classified as follows:
- Greenpeace is an outsider promotional group.
- The CBI is an insider sectional group.
- The NSPCC is an insider promotional and sectional group.
- The NFU is an insider sectional group.
- The Countryside Alliance is an outsider sectional and promotional group.

5 ■ Reduce the levels of tax avoidance and evasion.
- Labour and the Conservatives disagree on taxation levels for high income groups and the level of spending on the NHS.
- Two particular Liberal Democrat policies are constitutional reform and strong environmental protection measures.

6 ■ Momentum is left wing.
- Tory Reform Group is centrist.
- Conservative Way Forward is right wing.
- Liberal Democrats are centre-left.
- Blairites are also centre-left.

7 ■ The following parties won over 1 million votes in June 2017: Conservative; Labour; Liberal Democratic Party.

8 ■ The additional member system tends to produce the most proportional result.
- The single transferable vote gives most choice to voters.
- First past the post is most likely to produce an overall majority for the winner.

9 ■ The highest turnout was for the Scottish independence vote in 2014.
- The local referendums concerned the possible introduction of congestion charges.
- The devolution votes in 1997, the vote on Northeast devolution in 2004 and the vote on the Good Friday Agreement in 1998 were all regional.
- The rejection of devolution to Northeast England in 2004, a no majority of 55.8%.
- The narrowest majority was for Welsh devolution in 1997, a majority of 0.6%.

10 ■ (a) 78% of middle-class voters supported the Conservatives in 1964; (b) 43% of middle-class voters voted Conservative in 2017.
- (a) 64% of working-class voters supported Labour in 1964; (b) 59% of working-class voters supported Labour in 2017.
- The Conservatives have suffered more from class dealignment: support fell from 78% to 45%.

11 ■ 4% of the 18–24 age group voted Green in 2017.
- In the 65+ age group 59% voted Conservative in 2017, while 23% voted Labour.
- Support for the Conservative Party among 18–24-year-olds fell from 42% in 1979 to 18% in 2017.
- 65% of the BME community voted Labour in 2017, compared with 21% for the Conservatives.

12 ■ The least significant social factor is gender (virtually no difference).
- The most significant social factor is ethnicity.

13 ■ The Conservative defeat in 1997 was a combination of the disunity of the party, a recent economic recession and Labour being perceived to have a stronger leader (Blair versus Major).
- The Conservative/Liberal Democrat victory was largely about: Labour's perceived lack of economic competence, the financial crisis that was occurring, Labour's leader (Brown) being perceived to be indecisive and a strong anti-Labour media campaign.
- The Conservative victory in 2015 was largely about perceptions of leadership. Cameron was viewed more sympathetically than Clegg and Miliband. The Conservatives were also viewed as the most economically competent party.

14 ■ The Conservatives have most press support, both in terms of how many publications and the size of their circulation.
- The two most important Conservative-supporting papers are *The Sun* and the *Daily Mail*.
- The only mass circulation paper that supports Labour is the *Daily Mirror*.

Index